THE TOPKAPI SARAY MUSEUM

Carpets

The Topkapı Saray Museum

Carpets

translated, expanded and edited by
J. M. ROGERS
from the original Turkish by
HÜLYE TEZCAN

A New York Graphic Society Book
Little, Brown and Company · Boston

Publisher's note

This series of volumes dealing with the holdings of the Topkapı Saray Museum was originally undertaken by Dentsu Incorporated, Tokyo, in accordance with a cultural agreement between Turkey and Japan, with brief texts written by curators of the museum and translated into Japanese, and with photographs taken by Banri Namikawa. Dentsu published five volumes in 1980. This new edition, intended for a Western readership, was undertaken by Schuler Verlagsgesellschaft, Herrsching am Ammersee, under their own editorial control, following the terms of the license granted to them by Dentsu. The original authors (Filiz Çağman, Zeren Tanındı, Hülye Tezcan, Selma Delibaş and Cengiz Köseoğlu) are therefore responsible only for the texts in Japanese.

Photographs by BANRI NAMIKAWA

Text and notes on the illustrations based on original material by HÜLYE TEZCAN, translated from the Turkish, edited and expanded by J. M. ROGERS

This publication is adapted from and includes color plates first published in *Topkapı Sarayı Müzesi* (© 1980 Dentsu Incorporated, Tokyo) by the Topkapı Saray Museum Association, Tokyo, a subsidiary of Dentsu Incorporated
Copyright © 1987 by Schuler Verlagsgesellschaft mbH, Herrsching am Ammersee, West Germany

International Standard Book Number: 0–8212–1679–1
Library of Congress Catalog Card Number: 87–61700

First United States edition

New York Graphic Society books are published by Little, Brown and Company (Inc.)
Published simultaneously in Canada by Little, Brown & Company (Canada) Limited

Phototypeset in Great Britain
Text printed in West Germany
Illustrations printed in Japan
Bound in West Germany

Contents

Editor's note

The text of the present volume has been translated and adapted from the Turkish author's original version (prepared, with editorial co-ordination by the late Kemal Çığ, for the Japanese edition published in 1980); it has also been expanded by me for this edition, and many specific bibliographical citations have been added in the notes on the text at the end of individual chapters and, wherever appropriate, in the notes following captions to illustrations.

I am particularly grateful to Mr M. I. Waley of the British Library for his help with the Persian inscriptions and for his comments on the non-Koranic carpet inscriptions in general.

Transliteration
Differences in the phonetic structure of Arabic, Persian and Turkish make absolute consistency in transliteration impossible. The standard system used for Arabic (*Encyclopaedia of Islam*, 2nd ed.) with a few modifications works, in the editor's view, well enough for Persian. But for Ottoman Turkish, to make it easy for the reader to consult primary sources, account has been taken of the modern romanized Turkish alphabet: since Ottoman contains a large proportion of Arabic and Persian words, the effect is inevitably occasionally bizarre. There is, regrettably, no simple solution. Place names, however, are given in their modern form, without diacriticals.

J.M.R.

Foreword

FROM the later fifteenth century the Topkapı Saray was one of the principal residences of the Ottoman Sultans. Prior to the capture of Constantinople by Meḥmed II in 1453, their capitals were Bursa and Edirne, which they still continued to frequent seasonally. But after 1453 Constantinople, or, as it became known to the Ottomans, Istanbul – cheerfully distorted by the seventeenth-century historians to 'Islāmbol' (abounding in Islam) – was the seat of their empire.

The Great Palace of the Byzantine Emperors had disappeared centuries earlier and there was no large palace building standing which could readily be adapted to the requirements of Meḥmed the Conqueror. His first residence in Istanbul was the Eski Saray, between the ruined Byzantine Forum Tauri and the markets going down to the Golden Horn, but by the early 1470s he had left for the Acropolis of ancient Byzantium, a terrace dominating both the Sea of Marmara and the Golden Horn and enjoying vuews far up the Bosphorus. This would later be known as the Topkapı Saray, the Palace of the Cannon Gate. As well as being the Sultan's residence, with enormous kitchens, audience halls, grand reception rooms and separate quarters for the women, the complex of buildings was also, symbolically and in fact, the heart of an empire: its religious centre; the seat of the administration; the Treasury; and a vast storehouse of booty. It rapidly came to be a virtually self-sufficient entity, with mosques, schools, baths, Court workshops, libraries and prisons, and also included the Mint, Chancery (Divan), Armoury (housed in the Byzantine church of Haghia Eirene in the first courtyard of the palace), and a shrine (the Hırka-i Saadet Dairesi) for the relics brought back from Mecca and Medina by Selīm I (1512–20) – the whole being administered with the help of an enormous resident or semi-resident staff of servants, male and female attendants, guards, physicians and minor officials of all sorts.

While many of the first pavilions, as was Ottoman practice, were wooden and have since disappeared, that which now houses the Hazine (Treasury), built in 873/1468–9 on a high basement, was of cut stone. Like the three grand gateways of the Palace, it was there to impress, to give a suitable architectural setting for the ceremonies and splendours of the Sultan and his Court. The buildings added in the sixteenth and seventeenth centuries – with their rich marbles, tile-panels, inlaid wooden shutters, doors and panelling and their imposing calligraphy – skilfully combine strength and delicacy. Yet although each of them is the product of a personal whim or fantasy, the whole has a unity that makes the Topkapı Saray one of the most striking surviving palaces of Europe or Asia. Parts of it fell into decay or were torn down by later Sultans who wished for buildings more in the current style; much also was destroyed by the periodic fires. Since the Topkapı Saray became a museum in 1924, however, a programme of careful restoration has made it accessible to the public, some parts of it after centuries of neglect. The buildings, and their gardens and fountains, are thus now a living environment for the fabulously rich collections the palace contains and give the Topkapı Saray its unique position among the museums of the world.

These collections include a world-famous assemblage of Chinese porcelains, primarily booty in victorious Ottoman campaigns in Iran, Syria and Egypt in the earlier decades of the sixteenth century, but subsequently augmented by gifts from tributaries and allies. This is exhibited in the palace kitchens, which owe their distinctive appearance to restoration following a serious fire in 1574. There is also an important collection of clocks and watches, remaining from the European gifts of timepieces and mechanical instruments for which the Sultans had such a passion that they even demanded them as tribute. The Armoury included splendid examples of arms and armour made for, or even by, the Ottoman Sultans, together with prize pieces from Alexandria (captured in 1517) and Mongol, Turcoman and Safavid swords from victories at Başkent (1473) and Çaldiran (1514), as well as European arms and canonry. The richest spoils are, however, now in the Treasury and the Library – jewels, jewellery, hardstones and goldsmiths' work; and Korans, calligraphy and illustrated manuscripts and albums from Egypt, Syria, Mesopotamia, Iran, Central Asia and India: they are a tribute to the taste and discrimination of the conquering Ottoman rulers. Once in the Palace, moreover, they were not hoarded avariciously but inspired Ottoman craftsmen to emulate them. The finest creations of sixteenth- and seventeenth-century Ottoman art, as the collection of Royal textiles and their designs bears witness, owe much of their individuality to such prototypes imitated or skilfully adapted to traditional Turkish taste.

A number of carpets from the collections of the Topkapı Saray were considered worthy of inclusion in the famous exhibition of Islamic art held in Munich in 1910. Although renowned for other aspects of its vast collections, the Topkapı Saray is not known for its historic carpets, for the banal, if compelling, reason that carpets, unlike porcelains or goldsmiths' work, become worn out beyond the possibility of repair and have to be discarded: an old carpet, unlike a manuscript which no longer pleased its owner or a piece of cracked porcelain, was not even of use as a present. The costumes likewise must have worn out, and the surviving examples owe their preservation to the historical accident that on the death of a Sultan or a prince a considerable part of his wardrobe was bundled up and put away in the Palace stores. However, some of the garments were placed in royal tombs, as were carpets; most of these were collected together from the tombs and pious foundations of Istanbul in the 1880s, forming the nucleus of two world-famous carpet collections, that of the Türk ve Islâm Eserleri Müzesi (the Museum of Turkish and Islamic Art), now displayed in the palace of Ibrāhīm Paşa on the Hippodrome, and of the more recently opened Vakıflar Carpet Museum housed in the Sultan's apartments in the mosque of Sultan Aḥmed opposite. Not all these carpets, of course, would have been made or ordered for the Court in the first place, but they do provide the essential historical material for the appreciation of Ottoman Court taste in carpets which those in the Topkapı Saray collection, taken by themselves, can scarcely give.

Nevertheless, the Topkapı Saray carpets are of prime importance for the history of Court manufactures in Ottoman Turkey, particularly in the later years of the Ottoman Empire, the decorative arts of which period are often ignored. Indeed, they include a large group of handsome, finely woven, brilliantly coloured and lavishly inscribed prayer rugs which are unique in the history of carpet design. The indebtedness of their designs to Safavid ornament of the sixteenth century led them to be attributed formerly to Kashan, but it is now generally agreed that they are Ottoman manufactures of the nineteenth century, made in Istanbul, or possibly at Hereke. Their brilliant, eclectic revivalism throws an unfamiliar light on Ottoman taste in the nineteenth century – in porcelains, goldsmiths' work, embroidery or architectural decoration, for example – in which the influence of the European Rococo, Neoclassicism and even the Gothic Revival tends to be paramount, and demonstrates that at least in carpet-weaving the vigour of classical Ottoman art remained uncorrupted by the dubious standards of European Orientaliste art. The organization of the Palace workshops in the nineteenth century has so far been difficult to reconstruct and progress has been hampered by the infrequent publication of these carpets. Now, however, that for the first time it has been possible to consider them as a group, we may hope that this paradoxically dark age may be accorded the attention it deserves.

1

Ottoman Court workshops

MUCH has been made of the fact that lists of Palace craftsmen (*mevācib defterleri*) for the reigns of the Ottoman Sultans Bāyazīd II, Selīm I, Süleymān the Magnificent and Meḥmed III, and lists of seasonal gratuities, honoraria and rewards (*in'ām defterleri*) for the reign of Bāyazīd II (only partly published: similar registers from the Ottoman archives for certain years in the reign of Süleymān remain to be published) record both the existence of a Court carpet workshop[1] and the presentation of carpets by its head to the Sultan in the years 909–11 and 915 (1503–6 and 1509–10);[2] it goes without saying, however, that we have no idea whether these Court commissions differed in any way from the contemporary small- or large-pattern 'Holbeins' then being woven in Anatolia and exported to Italy and Northern Europe. Under Bāyazīd II the workshop may have numbered as many as nineteen craftsmen (including apprentices), but in the 932/1525–6 register, during the reign of Süleymān the Magnificent,[3] the numbers had gone down to six masters and ten apprentices. Later registers for Süleymān's reign show that the numbers of craftsmen continued to fluctuate. There is then a 30-year gap in the registers till the beginning of the reign of Meḥmed III. Then, suddenly, in the reign of Aḥmed I (1603–18) the workshop ceases to be mentioned in the register and its place is taken, at much lower daily wages, by a workshop of Imperial makers of turban-ornaments (*sōrğuçcuyān*). On the face of it, this was an extraordinary, if not inexplicable, development, suggesting a disaster in the Ottoman bureaucracy comparable to the abolition of a whole government department today. But even when the carpet workshop was in existence and operating in the earlier sixteenth century, there is much about its workings which seems strange or anomalous.

The successive registers for the earlier period allow us to trace the origins of the craftsmen, some of whom had first been employed as carpet-weavers under Meḥmed the Conqueror (1451–81), possibly the first Ottoman Sultan to have appointed carpet-weavers to his Court. Their daily wages were low and the weavers do not seem to have enjoyed annual increments, while their advancement from apprentice to master-craftsman was slow in the extreme; but nevertheless it is not really surprising to discover that membership of the workshop was to a large extent hereditary. The craftsmen included both *devşirme* boys from Central or Eastern Europe and slaves, from the *pencik*, the fifth part of the prisoners-of-war who fell to the Sultan's lot, as well as slaves presented to the Sultan or whose future was determined by the State on the death or disgrace of their previous owner and the confiscation of his estate. All those listed are Muslim, though some may have been renegades. On the whole, those stated to be slaves tend to fare rather less well in terms of daily wages: there is little evidence that any were manumitted in the course of their service, and even less that employment in a Court workshop eventually brought manumission as a matter of course.

Most interesting of all is the fact that recruitment to the workshop does not ever appear to have been either from nomads or from free carpet-weavers; and although it has often been asserted that Persian carpet-weavers were brought from Tabriz by Selīm I, following his victory at Çaldıran in 1514, or by Süleymān, in the wake of his victorious campaigns in Iraq and North-West Iran in 1535–5 and 1548, no carpet-weavers appear in a brief list of craftsmen conscripted from Tabriz in the early autumn of 1514 (Topkapı Saray Archives, D.10734); and none are described as Persian ('*Acem*) in the Palace registers of Süleymān's reign. Instead there are Croats, Circassians, Bosnians, Moreans, Wallachians, Russians, and craftsmen from Avloniya (Vallona), Niğbolu (Nico-polis ad Istrum in Bulgaria) and Kosovo. There is even a 'Firenk', probably an Italian, though he also was evidently converted to Islam, for he is listed as 'Firenk 'Osmān'.

Many of the craftsmen in other Court workshops listed in the registers of Süleymān's reign were of similar origins, and the history of carpet-weaving has never suggested that only craftsmen reared in a carpet-weaving tradition make good carpets. However, if we then match these lists of craftsmen with lists of gifts offered by craftsmen from the Court workshops and others to Süleymān on the great feasts of the Muslim year,[4] we discover that not one of the craftsmen mentioned in the Palace registers is recorded as offering a carpet; and not a single carpet appears to have been offered to Süleymān on these occasions by anyone else.

It must be said that although such Ottoman registers of craftsmen and of gifts offered by Court workshops to the Sultan suggest a highly refined bureaucratic organization, close inspection and comparison of them reveals numerous inconsistencies and demonstrates that their actual functioning may have been far from efficient. But the obvious conclusion in the present circumstances is that the craftsmen were there drawing their wages and doing nothing to earn them. How proper, one might feel today, that the workshop was abolished under Sultan Aḥmed; but equally, how extremely inefficient of the authorities not to have tumbled to the fact that the craftsmen were not giving value for money decades earlier. It must also be said, however, that this sort of gross inefficiency looks much more typical of the Ottoman bureaucracy than do the often exaggerated and romantic ideas of art-historians of the organization of the Court arts in sixteenth-century Turkey.

The only Palace treasury inventories of the sixteenth century are those from the reign of Bāyazīd II, and those of later centuries have not been accessible. That for the year 1505 (Topkapı Saray Archives, D.10026) has already been noticed in summary form.[5] It lists carpets from 'Menemen', near Manisa, in the old province of Saruhan: it may be prudent to retain the inverted commas for the moment, since the term may not be a provenance but a garbled form of the Arabic *munam-nam*, meaning 'decorated' or 'variegated'. Other carpets are described as *'Acem*, that is, broadly, from Persia, though since at this time Anatolia east of Kayseri was under strong Shīʿī or Kızılbas ('Alevī) influence, the so-called *'Acem* carpets could simply have been of Eastern Anatolian origin. There are, however, two other inventories which somewhat expand the contents of D.10026.[6] The first of these is undated and bears a heading which is difficult to accept as being strictly accurate, 'Eski defterden ziyade gelen esbabları bunlardır ki zikr olunur' (roughly, 'a list of objects supplementary to the old *defter*'). This may or may not be a reference to D.10026 but, somewhat mysteriously, some of the contents are not only identical but so odd (for example, 'some lion's claws in a piece of paper') that there can scarcely have been duplicate sets. This inventory (Topkapı Saray Archives, D.3/4)[7] anyway lists one silk carpet; sixteen Menemen carpets; an *'Acem* carpet made up of two pieces; and sixteen prayer rugs.

Since the term used here for silk, *ibrişim*, is otherwise used in these inventories for spun silk-embroidery thread, the 'silk' carpet referred to could have been embroidered and did not necessarily have a silk pile, warp or weft.

The second of these Treasury inventories (Topkapı Saray Archives, D.3/2), also evidently incomplete, though undated, includes two important groups of things with personal associations: belongings of Sultan Aḥmed, a son of Bāyazīd II who was a contender for the throne on his father's deposition in 1512 and who was despatched by his step-brother Selīm (Selīm I) in 1513; and belongings of the Safavid Shah Ismāʿīl, a rather heterogeneous lot and rather few too, which evidently were seized either at Çaldıran in 1514 or during the ensuing sack of Tabriz. This makes it possibly inappropriate to consider the inventory, despite its heading, as that of the Treasury of Bāyazīd II, though we may assume that Selīm I acquired all or most of it, with the result that the contents would be largely the same. The list of miscellaneous carpets here begins, appropriately enough, with a Heşt Bihişt carpet (*ḳālıçe-i Heşt Bihişt*), the 'Eight Paradises' and the name of the Safavid palace in Tabriz. This could very well have given its name to a type of (luxurious) carpet, but it may have been *the* Heşt Bihişt carpet, a famous round carpet placed under the central dome of the audience hall, described by an anonymous Venetian merchant who visited the palace late in the reign of the Akkoyunlu ruler, Yaʿqūb Beg.[8] The *'Acem* carpets include: a large room (sc. floor) carpet; a medium-sized Kirman carpet; a decorated (*münaḳḳaş*) carpet; a decorated silk (*ḥarīr*) carpet; and a small carpet of silk with gold metal thread (*ḳālıçe-i 'Acem 'an ḥarīr müzehheb küçik*). There was also a *KRWD* (possibly, Kurdish?) carpet. All or most of these may well have been spoils from Çaldıran or booty from Tabriz, for the earlier Ottoman Sultans are not known to have been avid collectors of Persian carpets. This group is supplemented by eighteen prayer rugs (*seccādehā-i 'Acem*), though in a section devoted to felt floor-coverings and possibly therefore of Persian felt (*keçe-i 'Acem*) too: this is a frequently recorded semi-luxury material in Ottoman inventories and fixed-price registers of the seventeenth century (cf. pp. 35f.).

The remaining carpets are still very few: a 'decorated Anatolian' carpet (*ḳālıçe-i Rūm bā naḳş*), whatever that may have been; a Menemen carpet; a room carpet with Menemen decoration (*ḳālıçe-i otāḳ bā naḳş-i Menemen* – perhaps just another Menemen carpet, not necessarily an imitation); and a Cairene carpet. This is a reminder that the white, red and striped felts which are listed immediately afterwards were for many decades the favourite type of floor-covering at practically all levels of Ottoman society. The ʿAcem prayer rugs are supplemented by another seventeen, of mohair or fine woollen felt (*tiftīk*). There are also 'Arabian' prayer carpets (*seccādehā-i ʿArabī*). The term, which may indicate the Hijaz as a provenance, is evidently intended to exclude Egypt and Cairo and may have been used only for cottons, some of the group being explicitly of cotton (*ālāca kirbās*) and some being of Yemeni striped cotton stuff (*ālāca-i Yemenī*). Ṣāmī (Syrian, Damascene) prayer rugs and those of *muṣannafkārī-i sefīd* (white, with a check pattern?) may also have been cotton, not felt or with a woollen pile.

Although the Treasury appears to have contained a respectable number of floor-coverings, there is little or nothing here which could be ascribed to the work of a Court workshop staffed by Central or Eastern European *devşirme* boys and prisoners-of-war: it shows, on the other hand, the extent to which the Ottoman palaces had recourse to the market, to loot or to tribute for much of their furnishings. This they almost certainly continued to do, nor is it at all likely that any of the Court workshops was set up, as if it were an exercise in Mercantilist theory, to cater for the sum of Court demand. But these inventories, like the Palace registers of the reign of Bāyazīd II, show that the Court carpet workshop played at best a background role, and that at a time when the complement of its staff appears to have been at its maximum.

There is, however, an alternative explanation to torpor, sloth or massive bureaucratic inefficiency for the persistence of the *ḳāliçebāfān-i Ḥāṣṣa* (Imperial carpet-weavers), to give them their Ottoman title, into the early seventeenth century. This is not unrelated to the concentration of carpet-weaving in Western and South-Western Anatolia and the Ottoman provinces (principally Cairo; Barbary is a less easily evaluated quantity, and though Damascus and Syria certainly produced rugs, there is no indication that they were for the Court and we have no idea of their appearance).[9] Indeed, the period 1480–1550 saw a revolution in the Ottoman carpet market, both in design and in dimensions, with a concentration of manufacturing activity in the Uşak area: new looms and of much larger size were set up, though the problems of re-adaptation may not in fact have been as great as might appear now to be the case, but certainly reorganization of labour was necessary, and possibly a considerable degree of conscription too. Halil Inalcık has recently suggested[10] that this development was a by-product of the Ottoman authorities' regulation of the Yürüks in Western Anatolia, who were under constant pressure to abandon their nomadic ways and become settled. How far the newly organized industry was centrally controlled as workshops in

urban centres and how much of it was run by merchants, possibly some of them State merchants,[11] who put out Court commissions to weavers in the villages or even in the summer pastures, is unclear: there was most probably a degree of both. The authorities certainly took charge of the financial organization, as one of the orders (dated 4 Cumādā II 960/19 April 1553) for the furnishing of the mosque of Süleymaniye in Istanbul (inaugurated 1557) shows.[12] This order was for a series of large carpets from the Uşak area and instructs the kadis of Tire, east of Ephesus, and of Güre, an outlying township of Uşak, to prepare a *nümüne defter* in connection with it: the term used insidiously suggests a *pattern book*, but it is most probably a calque on the contemporary German *Musterbuch*, used in the sense of account book.

All the evidence for State-encouraged carpet manufacture in the Uşak area in the mid- and later sixteenth century points to the fact that the authorities were not anxious to bring the weavers to Istanbul to set up their looms there. There was, however, one vital role which could scarcely be left to local labour or skills, namely the evolution of new designs and the maintenance of a degree of uniformity in the carpets woven. In terms of pattern, the carpets of these decades show two marked changes – in Anatolia, from the large- and small-pattern 'Holbeins' and arabesque or 'Lotto' carpets so much exported to Italy between 1450 and 1550, to the often enormous star- and medallion-Uşak carpets, which were reaching Europe by the 1530s; and in Egypt from the traditional Court carpets of 'Mamlūk' design to the elaborate Ottoman Court carpets and prayer rugs of the later sixteenth century or the large-medallion Court carpets of the seventeenth century. In each case there is demonstrably a degree of transition, suggesting that some of the changes may have been locally inspired or worked out in the course of manufacture. However, without the existence of centralized carpet design in Istanbul, the authorities would never have obtained the novelties they demanded. If there was a role which could have justified the continued existence of the Court carpet workshop attached to the Palace in Istanbul, it must have been the designing of carpets; although a design function need not necessarily have prevented the craftsmen from weaving carpets too, it may have been accepted by the Ottoman authorities as a good enough excuse for limiting the workshop's activities.

Julian Raby,[13] on the evidence of a letter from the Florentine factor Giovanni Maringhi in Pera dated 1501 complaining that the largest carpets of 9 *pichi* (the Florentine ell, used in measuring cloth) or more were almost unobtainable, draws attention to the shortage of large carpets on the Istanbul market in the early sixteenth century. The dearth may have been temporary, possibly reflecting local production difficulties, or the result of a sudden demand from Northern Italian merchants who had at last come to realize that only the largest carpets were imposing enough for Italian ceremonial, for grand marriages or to be spread out in churches in honour of a secular ruler or on the great feasts of the Christian church. It is also very likely, however, that the crisis of demand was not only from the export side and that demand for large carpets from the Ottoman Court was simultaneously increasing. Although at this time the Ottoman authorities are not known to have done anything to stifle foreign demand, they were, as always, in a good position to enforce their own priority. It should, however, be said that up to 1500 the small- and large-pattern 'Holbeins' popular in Italy do not appear to have been much used at the Ottoman Court, whatever their size.

The sixteenth-century 'design revolution' in Ottoman carpets may therefore have been a side effect of a growing Court demand for larger carpets. Not only do the star motifs and the medallions and corner-pieces of the large Uşak carpets recall basic forms of book illumination, but their curvilinear designs and grounds of floral trails demanded, at least in the initial stages, cartoons. Some of their motifs seem at first glance to be typically 'International Timurid', from the repertoire of stylized or formalized chinoiserie foliate or floral motifs that were, to a greater or lesser degree, characteristic of book illumination, from Edirne to Herat, in the mid- and later fifteenth century. Raby has, however, further shown[14] that the typical Uşak floral and foliate trails exploit a modified lotus-leaf, somewhat resembling an oak-leaf, which is peculiar to book-binding and illumination of the reign of Meḥmed the Conqueror and may have evolved, rather rapidly, between 1460 and 1475. Similar 'oak-leaves' also appear among sketches of foliate ornament in an album of designs from the end of Meḥmed's reign attributed to a certain Baba Nakkaş.[15] The medallion designs are also paralleled in contemporary bindings, and it is probable that the star designs of Uşak carpets derive from similar models, possible parallels being filigree medallions with arabesque filling from two other manuscripts made for Meḥmed the Conqueror, both now in the library of Süleymaniye (Süleymaniye 1025; Şehzāde Meḥmed 28) in Istanbul. Raby finds it difficult to explain exactly why the flora of the star-Uşaks became schematized so much more rapidly, but possibly, he suggests, their smaller size encouraged the craftsmen to abandon their cartoons at a comparatively early stage, thus losing contact with graphic models of decoration.

Elements of the Uşak peony- and lotus-trails then suggest to Raby that the cartoons themselves may have been drawn as early as 1475, implying that the earliest European representation of a star-Uşak in painting, in Paris Bordone's *Return of the Doge's ring by a fisherman* dated 1533 (Venice, Accademia), is of a type being made for the Ottoman Court by c.1500. This radical innovation in decoration, which seems to have largely excluded any transitional types, is, however, paralleled in the decoration of contemporary Iznik early blue-and-white pottery, first mentioned in the kitchen accounts of Meḥmed the Conqueror for 1469–73: this is a similarly daring adaptation of the 'International Timurid' decorative repertoire to cater for an unsatisfied demand by the Court for Chinese porcelains which, like all their contemporaries, the Ottomans admired but at the time could not get enough of. One might object that since book-binders' stamps were never thrown away and were constantly re-used or revived at the Ottoman Court, there could have been a considerable time-lag between the elaboration of ornament for the decoration of bindings and its adaptation for carpets and that the making of large Uşaks may therefore have begun somewhat later than 1480. But Raby rightly points out that there is little reason to believe that the carpets popular in Italy c.1500 necessarily reflected contemporary Ottoman Court taste, and that one should naturally expect a time-lag between a radical, high-fashion innovation for the Court and its availability to foreign merchants. In fact, by the time the enormous star- and medallion-Uşaks began to reach Europe in quantity in the later sixteenth century, Ottoman taste had turned to the elaborate Cairene Court designs, which in their way were revolutionary too.

To argue that it was the Palace carpet workshop which was responsible for the designs is to run counter to the generally accepted view that the designers responsible for adapting designs from illumination or book-binding were from the *nakkāşān*, i.e. the craftsmen employed by the Court on painted decoration for architecture, as well as on illumination and book illustration. Had such been the case, one is inclined to say, it would have made Ottoman Turkey unique among its contemporaries, in total contrast to Florence, for example, where contemporary designers like the Pollaiuolo family were craftsmen and executants as well, and where silk-designs in particular were the work of trained specialists. In fact, similar medallion-designs and similar foliate or floral motifs in illumination, book-binding, architectural decoration, tent-work, silks, leather-work and carpets all show considerable differences, not just of execution or of response to different materials, but of much more radical adaptation or reorganization. The assumption that the *nakkaşan* functioned at the Ottoman Court as a sort of design centre is thus dubious and anachronistic.

While the design of silks was almost certainly as autonomous at Bursa as it was in sixteenth-century Florence,[16] it is, of course, by no means so clear that there are similar technical requirements which entail that carpet cartoons have to be drawn up by specialists too. This therefore might in itself not be enough to justify the existence of the *ḳāliçebāfān-i Ḥāṣṣa*, though it was doubtless a considerable administrative convenience that the weavers could do the work. For it is extremely probable that each of the great Uşak carpets ordered in 1551 for the mosque of Sülemaniye needed a separate cartoon, so that any Palace designer would have been overstretched. We do not know either how large such drawings would have been: though Erdmann[17] has suggested that they would not have been full-size and could have been blown up by eye by the craftsmen working at the loom, the finer designs and the newer ones would have been more easily conveyed by means of full-size cartoons, which could then have been reduced by eye when a copy in smaller format was called for. Whether on-the-spot supervision by a member of the Court workshop was also necessary or whether control of quality was left to the head of the local workshop or to the authorities' financial representative, the kadi, is unknown.

Some corroboration of this admittedly somewhat conjectural explanation of the continued appearance of the Palace carpet-weavers in the Palace registers may be found in practice in sixteenth-century Egypt, where Selīm I's conquest of 1516–17 seems first to have made the famous products of the Cairo looms available to the Court in Istanbul; and where the numerous surviving Mamlūk carpets show that they had made a speciality of producing large pieces. The rise and evolution of the 'Mamlūk' style has occasioned much discussion since, although the fifteenth-century Cairene historian, al-Maqrīzī,[18] in his account of the sack of the palace of Qūsūn in 1341 refers to pairs of (Cairene) carpets valued at 12,000 silver coins each – not to mention *busut*, possibly flat-woven, from Rūm (Anatolia), Āmid (Diyarbekir) and Shiraz – practically none of the extant Mamlūk rugs can plausibly be dated much before 1500.

It is now generally accepted that the carpets variously described in Italian inventories, bills of lading and other documents of the fifteenth–sixteenth centuries as 'Damascene', 'Alexandrian' and 'Cairene' must all have been made in Cairo. It was, however, long taken for granted that Selīm I's conquest of Egypt brought Egyptian industry to an immediate and annihilating

close, but the work of Kühnel and Erdmann[19] on Cairene carpets, which identified a group of hybrid or transitional 'Mamlūk'–Ottoman pieces, was an indication that such a collapse was a fiction, doubtless based on the exaggerated claims of the contemporary Egyptian historians. This has been triumphantly corroborated in the present decade by the discovery, in the Palazzo Pitti in Florence, of a 'Mamlūk' carpet of enormous size, evidently made c.1541, which arrived in the Medici collections between 1557 and 1571.[20] The carpet is still in almost perfect condition, which means that it must have been new at the time of its acquisition. Because of its size this carpet must have been a special commission, which raises the possibility that its characteristically 'Mamlūk' design was by that time rather old-fashioned. It is, however, a clear demonstration that the so-called 'Mamlūk' style was vigorous and persistent, and suggests that the 'very large' (*ğāyet büyük*) carpets ordered from Egypt in the 1550s for the mosque of Süleymaniye in Istanbul were of comparable size and similar appearance. The Cairene looms obviously continued to make large pieces, like the Medici 'Ottoman' carpet which reached their collections in 1622,[21] but the second 'design revolution' relates in fact not to the carpets of such size, which were evidently overtaken by the giant Uşaks of the mid-sixteenth century, but to smaller carpets and prayer rugs, of elaborate and beautiful design, which are generally known as Ottoman 'Court' carpets.

This term is evidently no misnomer, though it rests on a misinterpretation of a well-known order of the reign of Murād III, dated 3 Zilka'de 993/27 October 1585,[22] for craftsmen to be sent from Cairo, together with a quantity of dyed wool: this demand has led many commentators to conclude that about this date a special Court manufacture was established at Istanbul – or possibly Bursa – where the 'Court' carpets are thought consequently to have been made. To reject this is not, of course, to deny that carpets were ever woven in these two Ottoman capitals – though for the sixteenth and early seventeenth centuries, if any were it has not yet been possible to identify them – but to point out that this is not what the 1585 order either means or implies. Demands for craftsmen from Cairo could well have come regularly, as much as two or three times a year, for checks on their work, possibly, by the *ḳāliçebāfān-i Ḥāṣṣa* (none of them, doubtless significantly, Cairene by origin), or possibly for instruction in the execution of new and complex designs. Still less does the 1585 order mean that from that year onwards fine carpets ceased to be made in Cairo.

What does appear to be the case is that the novel Court carpets woven in Cairo needed cartoons, followed

Istanbul taste in design, required a good deal of supervision and may have been made as early as the 1550s. There are still a considerable number of such carpets extant, showing a wide degree of variation upon a number of basic designs, most of which would have entailed the use of redrawn cartoons, at least for elements of the design – borders, medallions, spandrels, corner-pieces, etc. Those which have evoked most comment are compositions of naturalistic floral ornament or of cloud-scrolls, flowering Prunus branches, peony- and lotus-scrolls and feathery leaves (often known as *ṣāz*, in old Turkish 'reed' or 'jungle'), of which the border of *No. 1* in the present volume – a carpet removed in 1885 from the tomb of either Selīm I (1512–21) or Selīm II (1566–74) in Istanbul, but often said to have been the prayer carpet of Sultan Aḥmed I – is a good example. Some of the larger carpets of this type have designs organized symmetrically on both axes,[23] but the most elaborate examples are prayer carpets with a vertically symmetrical field of fantastic foliage adapted or elaborated from line drawings in albums made for Süleymān the Magnificent, Selīm II or Murād III between 1560 and 1580. These drawings, and slightly more distant resemblances to tile panels in the mosque of Rüstem Paşa (died 1561) or in the Harem apartments in the Topkapı Saray added by Murād III between 1575 and 1578, which are similarly designed as niches, have been a principal reason for the now widespread belief that all of them – drawings, tile panels and carpet designs – were the work of the same hand in the Palace scriptorium. The resemblances are, however, not the result of a single organizing intellect but of the simple fact that prayer carpets and Iznik tile panels perform very similar functions, indicating the direction of Mecca, so that one will appropriately recall the other; but, this fundamental similarity apart, there are no exact copies and considerably greater differences than one might expect. As for the line drawings in the Palace albums; these are virtuoso mannerist compositions, the effect of which depends entirely upon contrasts of line or modelling; they were not intended to be reproduced elsewhere, nor would they have been so successful. The few carpets, like one (*c.*1570–80) in the Walters Art Gallery, Baltimore, which base their design upon such fantastic foliage, have been totally redrawn, and the foliate forms have been simplified adroitly to transform contrasts of line into colour contrasts. If the cartoons were the work of a single draughtsman, there is nothing to show it, whereas the careful accentuation of the vertical axis in the Court carpets indicates concern for the practicalities of weaving. Why should this adaptation not be the work of the specialized *ḳāliçebāfān-i Ḫāṣṣa*?

The depiction of great Uşak carpets in Italian and Northern European painting of the later sixteenth century shows that foreigners, probably quite regularly, broke into the Court economy, possibly by suborning the weavers and offering them the chance to moonlight, or by buying up orders on the spot which had become surplus to local requirements. Moonlighting, in the case of a large carpet which could take many months to complete, would have been too easy to detect, and the problems of capitalization during the weaving may have made such work less attractive to the craftsmen. There is even more interesting evidence, however, of foreign penetration of the Cairo looms for the weaving of Court carpets in the form of prayer rugs with Hebrew inscriptions (not all of them, however, perfectly executed). That recently published[24] from a Padua synagogue has been shown to be a completely new departure, for it is not a floor carpet and still less a prayer carpet, despite its niche, but in fact a curtain for the Ark of the Covenant. It bears in Hebrew a verse from the Psalms (118, 20), 'This is the gate of the Lord, through which the righteous shall enter.' and has been designed after the title page of a printed Haggadah of *c.*1550–75, probably from Northern Italy but possibly printed in Istanbul, though with a number of transitional 'Mamlūk'–Ottoman elements. It is likely, though not certain, that this piece also would have been woven after a cartoon. Would such a cartoon incorporating a Hebrew inscription have been drawn by someone in the Palace? Though none of the *ḳāliçebāfān-i Ḫāṣṣa* is listed as Jewish, craftsmen in other Court workshops certainly were, and it is clear that Jews were not excluded on religious grounds from employment at the Court. It could also be an interesting, though extremely rare, case of a private commission from some Court employee. Alternatively, there could have been a Jewish or Italian merchant in Cairo with an ability to explain to the weaver just what he wanted.

Not, however, that the Padua synagogue curtain need have been made in Cairo at all, for there is good evidence that 'Oriental' carpets were also being woven in contemporary Italy. These were not the copies of Uşaks being woven all over Europe, from England to the Ukraine, but the work of Near Eastern craftsmen. There is a letter from Barbara of Brandenburg in 1464 to an acquaintance in Istanbul asking for a Turkish female slave to weave carpets, and it has been suggested by Rodolfo Signorini, in his recent study of the Camera Dipinta in the Gonzaga palace at Mantua, that the carpet shown in Mantegna's famous fresco may actually have been her work. There was also a workshop under Alfonso d'Este at Ferrara from 1490 directed by 'Sabadino Moro' (evidently a Muslim, Sabāḥ al-Dīn)[25] who moved there from Cairo and opened a workshop employing many weavers. None of his carpets survives, but an inventory of 1529 lists a table rug of wool and silk decorated with *fregi et compassi* (friezes and roundels), and he possibly also made the 'magnificent carpet' bequeathed by Alfonso in his will (23 August 1533) to Bona of Poland. If he had a designer, the fact is not recorded, and he may have been his own designer. Presumably he would have been under less pressure to innovate at the Court of Ferrara than were the Cairene weavers for the Ottoman Court. Nor do we know whether Sabadino used wool from Cairo, but he evidently satisfied the exigent demands of the Northern Italian princely states, at least for adroit copies of grand carpets imported with difficulty from Cairo or Alexandria.

What became of the Cairo carpet looms in the seventeenth century? The prices of Cairene carpets in the 1640 Istanbul fixed-price register (cf. pp. 35f.) are moderate and suggest that those available on the Istanbul market were of no better than middling quality. What may well have happened is that the growing taste for Persian carpets which shows itself in Ottoman Turkey towards 1600 became dominant and led to a marked decline in Court orders for carpets from Uşak and Cairo. This would also reasonably explain the suppression of the *ḳāliçebāfān-i Ḥāṣṣa* under Aḥmed I and the replacement of weavers by makers of turban-ornaments. Palace-designed carpet manufactures were superseded by recourse to the trade in Persian carpets, and it was quite possibly thought to be cheaper or less complicated to buy Anatolian rugs for the Court from the trade too. There are reminiscences of the 'Cairene Court' carpets in prayer rugs of the late seventeenth and early eighteenth centuries from Gördes, Bergama and Lâdik, though it is far from clear that these were made for the Court. One might conclude that, when the weavers saw their livelihood vanishing, they turned to manufacture for the wider market, still keeping to well-tried traditional patterns at a time when Imperial fashion had changed and was in the thrall of exotic, fancy, Persian styles.

For all that has recently been said about the Court workshops as centres of excellence in the Ottoman Empire,[26] the rise and decline of the Court carpet-weavers may well have represented a typical situation: unsystematically recruited; quite probably under-employed for much of the time; underpaid like all the craftsmen listed in the Palace registers (for most of the sixteenth century the daily stipend of the *Ḥāṣṣa* was constant, in spite of severe inflation, and at 1–3 akçe *per diem* for an apprentice it was well below a living wage); and, when Court fashion changed, instead of being set to supply the new fashion, unceremoniously suppressed. But this was not exactly the end of the story, for there is in the Topkapı Saray a group of inscription carpets which have given rise to the most various attributions. Though they are now generally agreed to have been made in the nineteenth century, possibly even towards the end of the century, it is highly probable that they represent the products of a Court workshop. Paradoxically, we know very little indeed of the organization of the Ottoman *Kunstindustrie* in the late years of the Empire, and the craftsmen and their origins remain a mystery. But just as the carpets themselves are striking products of revivalism in late Ottoman art, we may guess that the organization of the workshop itself was a piece of revivalism on the bureaucratic level. It is to these that we must now turn.

NOTES TO CHAPTER 1

1 Bige Çetintürk, 'Istanbul'da XVI asır sonuna kadar hâssa halı sanatkârları. I. Türk san'at eserleri ve halı hakkında mutalealar', *Türk San'atı Tarihi Araştırma ve Incemeleri* I (Istanbul 1963), 716–31. The documents here cited are: Topkapı Saray Archives, D.9613–2, datable pre-932/1525–6; D.9613–1, dated 932/1525–6; D.9613–3, dated Maṣar 952/March-June 1545; D.9612, covering the period Muḥarram 965 to Muḥarram 966/October 1557–October 1558; Başbakanlık Arşivi Maliye, D.6196, dated Maṣar 974/July-October 1566; Topkapı Saray Archives, D.9613–13, dated Reşen 1004/March-May 1596; and D.9613–15, dated Maṣar 1005/August-November 1596. There are other relevant documents, still unpublished, in the Başbakanlık Archives.
2 So far only published in full for the year 909/26 June 1503–13 June 1504: Ö. L. Barkan, 'Istanbul saraylarına ait muhasebe defterleri', *Belgeler* IX (Ankara 1979), 296–380. The most valuable, or most highly rewarded, carpet presented to the Sultan in this year, however, was not from the head of the carpet workshop.
3 I. H. Uzunçarşılı, 'Osmanlı Saray'ında ehl-i hiref (sanatkârlar) defteri', *Belgeler* IX (Ankara 1981–86), 23–76.
4 Rıfkı Melûl Meriç, 'Bayramlarda Padişahlara hediye edilen san'at eserleri ve karşılıkları. Türk san'atı tarihi vesikaları', *Türk San'atı Tarihi Araştırma ve Incemeleri* I (Istanbul 1963), 764–86; I. H. Uzunçarşılı, art. cit. (note 3).
5 J. M. Rogers, 'An Ottoman Palace inventory of the reign of Bayazid II', in *VIᵉ Colloque du CIEPO, Cambridge 1984*, ed. J. L. Bacqué-Grammont (Istanbul 1986); cf. J. M. Rogers (ed.), *The Topkapı Saray Museum. The Treasury* (London and Boston, Mass. 1987), 21.
6 Cf. Julian Raby and Ünsal Yücel, 'The archival documentation: 1. The scope of the documents; 2. The earliest Treasury registers' in

Chinese Ceramics in the Topkapi Saray Museum. A complete catalogue: I. Historical Introductions, Yuan and Ming dynasty Celadon Wares, Regina Krahl, in collaboration with Nurdan Erbahar, ed. John Ayers (London 1986), 65–81. The authors rightly draw attention to the more systematic appearance of D.3/4 and D.3/2, but this is largely deceptive; there is some reason, indeed, for thinking that D.3/4, despite its heading, was a preliminary draft for D.10026.

7   J. M. Rogers, 'Plate and its substitutes in Ottoman inventories' in Michael Vickers (ed.), *Pots and Pans* (Oxford 1986), 117–36.

8   C. Grey (ed.), *A narrative of Italian travels in Persia in the fifteenth and sixteenth centuries* (Hakluyt Society, London 1873), 175. The writer mistakenly attributes the palace to Uzūn Ḥasan, who died in 1478.

9   Cf. the evidence of Emmanuel Piloti, who was in Egypt for much of the period 1396–1438. P. H. Dopp (ed.), *Traité d'Emmanuel Piloti sur le passage en Terre Sainte (1420)* (Louvain 1950).

10   Halil Inalcık, 'The Yürüks: Their origins, expansion and economic role' in Robert Pinner and W. B. Denny (eds.), *Carpets of the Mediterranean countries 1400–1600* (London 1986), 39–65.

11   J. M. Rogers, 'Ottoman luxury trades and their regulation' in *Osmanistische Studien zur Wirtschafts- und Sozialgeschichte. In Memoriam Vančo Boškov*, ed. H.-G. Majer (Wiesbaden 1986), 135–55; Suraiya Faroqhi, 'Textile production in Rumeli and the Arab provinces: Geographical distribution and internal trade', *Osmanlı Araştırmaları/The Journal of Ottoman Studies* I (1980), 61–83.

12   Ö. L. Barkan, *Süleymaniye Camii ve Imareti Inşaatı* II (Ankara 1979), 194, Nos. 496–7; J. M. Rogers, 'The State and the arts in Ottoman Turkey. 2. The furnishing and decoration of Süleymaniye', *International Journal of Middle East Studies* 14 (1982), 283–313.

13   Julian Raby, 'Court and export. Part 1. Market demands in Ottoman carpets 1450–1550' in *Carpets of the Mediterranean countries*, op. cit. (note 10), 29–38.

14   Id., 'Court and export. Part 2. The Uşak carpets' ibid., 177–87.

15   In the Istanbul University Library. Cf. S. Ünver, *Fâtih devri saray nakışhanesi ve Baba Nakkaş çalışmaları* (Istanbul 1958).

16   Florence Edler de Roover, 'Andreas Banchi. Florentine silk-manufacturer and merchant in the fifteenth century', *Studies in Medieval and Renaissance History* III (Lincoln, Nebraska 1966), 223–85; J. M. Rogers, art. cit. (note 11).

17   K. Erdmann, 'Carpet cartoons' in *Seven Hundred Years of Oriental Carpets*, ed. Hanna Erdmann, trans. May H. Beattie and Hildegard Herzog (London 1970), 187–9.

18   Cited in R. G. Irwin, 'Egypt, Syria and their trading partners 1450–1550' in *Carpets of the Mediterranean countries*, op. cit. (note 10), 73–82.

19   E. Kühnel and L. Bellinger, *Cairene carpets and others technically related* (Washington, D.C. 1957); K. Erdmann, 'Kairener Teppiche. I. Europäische und islamische Quellen des 15–18. Jahrhunderts', *Ars Islamica* V (1938), 179–206; 'II. Mamlūken- und Osmanenteppiche', *Ars Islamica* VII (1940), 55–81; id., 'Neuere Untersuchungen zur Frage der Kairener Teppiche', *Ars Orientalis* IV (1961), 65–105; Şerare Yetkin, 'Osmanlı Saray halılarından yeni örnekler', *Sanat Tarihi Yıllığı* VII (1977), 143–64. Erdmann suggests that the export of Cairene 'Mamlūk' rugs must have increased considerably in the years after 1528 when European merchants were permitted to reside in Cairo.

20   *The Eastern carpet in the Western world from the fifteenth to the seventeenth century*, exhibition catalogue (London 1983), No. 21; Alberto Boralevi, 'Three Egyptian carpets in Italy' in *Carpets of the Mediterranean countries 1400–1600*, op. cit. (note 10), 205–20.

21   *The Eastern carpet in the Western world* ... (op. cit.), No. 56; Boralevi, art cit. (note 20).

22   W. B. Denny, 'The origin and development of Ottoman Court carpets' in *Carpets of the Mediterranean countries 1400–1600*, op. cit. (note 10), 243–59.

23   M. Dimand and Jean Mailey, *Oriental rugs in the Metropolitan Museum of Art* (New York 1973), No. 103, MMA 41.190.257. Dimand's ascription of all such carpets to workshops in 'Bursa or Istanbul' has so far had no evidence to substantiate it.

24   A. Boralevi, 'Un tappeto ebraico italo-egiziano', *Critica d'Arte* XLIX (1984), 34–47.

25   A. Venturi, 'Le arti minori a Ferrara nella fine del secolo XV. L'arazzeria', *L'Arte* XII (1909), 207–10; G. Campori, 'L'arazzeria estense', *Atti e Memorie delle RR deputazioni di storia patria per le provincie di Modena e Parma* VIII (1876), 427–8, 465.

26   Esin Atıl, *The Age of Süleyman the Magnificent*, exhibition catalogue (Washington, D.C. 1987).

2

The inscription carpets

Introduction

ONE of the most conspicuous carpet groups illustrated in the present volume (*Nos. 2–35*) is principally represented in the collections of the Topkapı Saray, which has at least thirty-seven examples. Others, in museums and private collections in Europe and the United States, mostly have an Istanbul provenance or are reported to have been gifts from the Ottoman Sultans. Their high quality, brilliant colours, often boldly enhanced with brocaded metal thread, their extremely varied designs and their fine condition leave no doubt that these carpets were Palace commissions. They first seem to have attracted the attention of connoisseurs and collectors in the 1880s, and since that time have been published with the most diverse, and often unconvincing, attributions: even in recent catalogues there is little general agreement, while discrepancies in their technical descriptions make it difficult to decide whether several pieces were woven to a particular design, but with warps, wefts and piles of various materials; or whether the writers did not have a proper opportunity to get their facts right. Though the Persian knot was used for practically all these carpets, there is general agreement now that the group is of Turkish origin, but the location of the looms and the chronology of their manufacture remain to be discovered. It is also generally agreed that the carpets are by no means as old as they were first thought to be. Even if they turn out to be of relatively recent manufacture, however, they are still of considerable cultural importance on account of the abundance of the inscriptions they bear, a feature which makes them a unique phenomenon in the history of carpet-weaving.

The texts of the inscriptions

With the possible exception of the two round cartouches in the spandrels of one carpet reproduced in the present volume (*No. 2*), which, it has unconvincingly been claimed, may include a craftsman's signature, '*amal Maḥmūd al-Kirmānī*, all the published inscriptions on carpets of this Topkapı Saray group are Koranic, or *du'ā* (short prayers, pious sayings, blessings upon God or His Prophet, etc.), or lists or invocations of the *Asmā' Allāh al-Ḥusnā* (known as the '99 Names of God', though there are actually more than a hundred of them). Exceptionally, some of the cartouches of square Kufic (as seen, for example, in *No. 8*) or panels above mihrabs (for example, *No. 27*) may be *ḥadīth*, though the Traditions have not been identified or even, in the former case, read. Some of the *du'ā* is Persian, not Arabic. That appearing on the panel above the mihrab in *No. 26* is a reminiscence of Koran III, 32–3 –

> And when she [the wife of Imran] was delivered of it, she said, LORD, verily I *have* brought forth a female (and GOD well knew what she had brought forth), and a male is not as a female: I have called her Mary; and I commend her to thy protection, and *also* her issue, against Satan driven away with stones. Therefore the Lord accepted her with a gracious acceptance, and caused her to bear an excellent offspring. And Zacharias took care of *the child*; whenever Zacharias went into the chamber to her, he found provisions with her: *and* he said, O Mary, whence hadst thou this? she answered, This is from God; for GOD provideth for whom he pleaseth without measure.

– in verse or rhyming prose. Other Persian inscriptions, however, like the outer and inner inscriptions seen in *Nos. 15, 16* and *32*, could best be described as *munājāt*, or mystical communing, i.e. invocation or apostrophe of the Deity, in high-flown but informal or non-canonical prose. Such prayers do not appear to have been collected, hence it is at present difficult to draw any conclusions of substance from their presence. The Arabic *du'ā* inscriptions are broadly comparable to the prayers in such standard manuals as the *Dalā'il al-Khayrāt* of al-Jazūlī, the eighteenth-century Moroccan Sufi, a work which was widely popular in the Ottoman Empire.

The inscription carpets

The texts quoted below show that the Koranic inscriptions are all more or less appropriate to the theme of prayer, but they also demonstrate the decidedly idiosyncratic ideas of the rug designers. In fact, most of the rugs bear extracts from Suras rather than continuous texts, and in some cases as many as seven or eight such extracts at a time. In some examples where space remains at the end of a Koranic verse (*āya*), the calligrapher has continued with the following verse, breaking it off abruptly, however, when the available space was used up. In others such spaces are filled with *du'ā* or a selection of the '99 Names of God'. Some of the texts, moreover (for example, the outer inscription band, Koran II, 256, seen in *No. 35*), have lacunae. Such lacunae could be the result of an oversight on the calligrapher's part, like the occasional dittography of words or phrases in other inscriptions; or they could be evidence of a slapdash attempt to reassure the faithful that the inscription in question included the whole of the verse. Neither truncation nor such lacunae met with orthodox approval, but faults of this kind are so common in Arabic epigraphy that often the orthodox cannot have noticed them. Unlike a written page of a Koran, moreover, on which a mistake in the text could be erased or corrected not too obtrusively, there was in practice little to be done to correct a mistake in a woven inscription, the only solution being to destroy the offending carpet. Inconspicuous mistakes may therefore have been tacitly accepted or passed by the head of the workshop.

The verses quoted below are cited after Sale's translation of the Koran (London 1734, and many more recent editions):

II, 255 [the Āyat al-Kursī]

O true believers, give *alms* of that which we have bestowed on you, before the day cometh wherein there shall be no merchandizing, nor friendship, nor intercession. The infidels are unjust doers. GOD! there is no GOD but he; the living, the self-subsisting: neither slumber nor sleep seizeth him; to him *belongeth* whatsoever is in heaven, and on earth. Who is he that can intercede with him, but through his good pleasure? He knoweth that which is past, and that which is to come unto them, and they shall not comprehend anything of his knowledge, but so far as he pleaseth. His throne is extended over heaven and earth and the preservation of both is no burden unto him. He is the High, the Mighty.

II, 256

Let there be no violence in religion. Now is right direction manifestly distinguished from deceit; whoever therefore shall deny Tagut [i.e. idols], and

believes in God, he shall surely take hold on a strong handle, which shall not be broken; GOD is he who heareth and seeth.

II, 257

GOD is the patron of those who believe; he shall lead them out of darkness into light; but *as to* those who believe not, their patrons are Tagut; they shall lead them from the light into darkness; and they shall be the companions of hell fire, they shall remain therein for ever.

II, 285

The apostle believeth in that which hath been sent down unto him from his LORD, and the faithful *also*. Every one *of them* believeth in GOD, and his angels, and his scriptures, and his apostles. And they say, We have heard, and do obey: *we implore* thy mercy, O LORD, for unto thee must we return. GOD will not force any soul beyond its capacity: it shall have *the good* which it gaineth, and it shall suffer *the evil* which it gaineth.

II, 286

O LORD, punish us not, if we forget, or act sinfully: O LORD, lay not on us a burden like that which thou has laid on those who have been before us; neither make us, O LORD, to bear what we have not strength to *bear*, but be favourable unto us, and spare us, and be merciful unto us. Thou art our patron, help us therefore against the unbelieving nations.

III, 18–20

GOD hath borne witness that there is no GOD but he; and the angels, and *those who are* endowed with wisdom, *profess the same*; who executeth righteousness; there is no GOD but he; the Mighty, the Wise. Verily the *true* religion in the sight of GOD, is Islam; and they who had received the scriptures dissented not *therefrom*, until after the knowledge *of God's unity* had come unto them out of envy among themselves; but whosoever believeth not in the signs of GOD, verily GOD will be swift in *bringing him* to account. If they dispute with thee, say, I have resigned myself unto GOD, and he who followeth me *doth the same*: and say unto them who have received the scriptures and to the ignorant. Do ye profess *the religion of* Islam? Now if they embrace Islam, they are surely directed; but if they turn their backs, verily unto thee *belongeth* preaching *only*; for GOD regardeth his servants.

IV, 103

And when ye shall have ended *your* prayer, remember GOD, standing, and sitting, and *lying* on your sides. But when ye are secure *from danger*, complete *your* prayers; for prayer is commanded the faithful, *and* appointed *to be said* at the stated times.

VI, 83–4
And this is our argument wherewith we furnished Abraham *that he might make use of it* against his people: we exalt unto degrees of *wisdom and knowledge* whom we please; for thy LORD is wise *and* knowing. And we gave unto him Isaac and Jacob; we directed *them* both; and Noah had we before directed and of his posterity David and Solomon; and Job, and Joseph, and Moses, and Aaron: thus do we reward the righteous.

VII, 204–6
And when the Koran is read, attend thereto, and keep silence; that ye may obtain mercy. And meditate on thy LORD in thine own mind, with humility and fear and without loud speaking, evening and morning; and be not one of the negligent. Moreover *the angels*, who are with my LORD, do not proudly disdain his service, but they celebrate his praise and worship him.

XI, 88
He said, O my people, tell me; if I have received an evident declaration from my LORD, and he hath bestowed on me an excellent provision, and I will not consent unto you in that which I forbid you; do I seek *any other* than *your* reformation, to the utmost of my power? *My support is from* GOD *alone; on him do I trust, and unto him do I turn me.*

XIV, 40–1
O LORD, grant that I may be an observer of prayer, and *a part* of my posterity *also*, O LORD; and receive my supplication, O LORD, forgive me, and my parents, and the faithful, on the day whereon an account shall be taken.

XVII, 78–9
And thou shalt not find any change in our *prescribed* method. Regularly perform *thy* prayer at the declension of the sun, at the first darkness of the night, and the prayer of daybreak; for the prayer of daybreak is borne witness unto *by the angels.* And watch *some part* of the night in the same *exercise*, as a work of supererogation for thee; peradventure thy LORD will raise thee to an honourable station.

XXI, 87
And *remember* Dhu'lnun [i.e. Jonah, who was swallowed by the whale] when he departed in wrath, and thought that we could not exercise our power over him.

And he cried out in the darkness, *saying, There is no* GOD, *besides thee: praise be unto thee! Verily I have been one of the unjust.*

XXIV, 35
GOD is the light of heaven and earth: the similitude of his light is as a niche in a wall, wherein a lamp *is placed, and* the lamp *enclosed* in a *case of* glass; the glass *appears* as it were a shining star. It is lighted with *the oil of* a blessed tree, an olive neither of the east, nor of the west: it wanteth little but that the oil thereof would give light, although no fire touched it. *This is* light *added* unto light: GOD will direct unto his light whom he pleaseth. GOD propoundeth parables unto men; for GOD knoweth all things.

XXVII, 30
It is from Solomon, and *this* is the *tenour thereof*: In the name of the most merciful GOD, Rise not up against me: but come, and surrender yourselves unto me.

XXXIII, 56
Verily GOD and his angels bless the prophet: O true believers, do ye *also* bless him, and salute *him* with *a respectful* salutation.

LIX, 23–4
He is GOD, besides whom there is no GOD; who knoweth that which is future and that which is present: he *is* the most Merciful; he is GOD, besides whom there is no GOD: the King, the Holy, the Giver of peace, the Faithful, the Guardian, the Powerful, the Strong, the most High. Far be GOD exalted above *the idols*, which they associate *with him*! He is GOD, the Creator, the Maker, the Former. He hath most excellent names. Whatever *is* in heaven and earth praiseth him: and he *is* the Mighty, the Wise.

LXVIII, 51–2
It wanteth little but that the unbelievers strike thee down with their *malicious* looks, when they hear the admonition *of the Koran*; and they say, He *is* certainly distracted: but it *is* no other than an admonition unto all creatures.

CVIII, 1–3
IN THE NAME OF THE MOST MERCIFUL GOD.
Verily we have given thee Al Cawthar [i.e. abundance]. Wherefore we pray unto thy LORD; and slay the victims. Verily he who hateth thee shall be childless.

CXII, 1–4
IN THE NAME OF THE MOST MERCIFUL GOD.
Say, *God* is one God; the eternal God: he begetteth not,

neither is he begotten and there is not any one like unto him.

———————

The mere fact that each carpet in this group is inscribed is itself worthy of remark, for there has traditionally been prejudice in Islam against inscriptions underfoot. This factor doubtless explains the thinking behind the use of pseudo-Kufic borders both on the Anatolian 'Seljuk' carpets from Konya and Beyşehir and on many 'Holbein' and 'Lotto' rugs, though the forms these pseudo-Kufic borders may take probably derive from thirteenth-century Anatolian Seljuk architectural decoration. It also explains the habit of the faithful of picking up any scrap of paper with writing on it which may be lying on the ground, in case it bears Holy Writ or the name of God, and secreting such scraps in cracks in walls. To this amiable, if pietistic, practice we owe sometimes whole archives of documents, like those from the Nubian fortress of Qasr Ibrim in Upper Egypt, recently published.[1] Pietism seems moreover, to have gone occasionally even further, discouraging the inclusion even of isolated letters or profane inscriptions upon carpets, for these would have had the potentiality of being arranged or rearranged to form the word 'Allāh' or one of the '99 Names of God'.

It is clear from the inscribed Kashan and Tabriz carpets of the sixteenth century that such pietism was not characteristic of the Safavid Court, or possibly even of the Shī'a in general: this may lend particular significance to the occasional occurrence on the carpets of this group in the Topkapı Saray of inscriptions which are Shī'ī in tone. Most of the sixteenth-century inscriptions are anyway not Koranic but, as on a Tabriz carpet in the Topkapı Saray (cf. *No. 46*), examples of Persian lyric poetry,[2] celebrating the joys of love, youth, spring and wine, and hence possibly so infuriated the '*ulamā*' (theologians and Islamic lawyers) that their *pietistic* disapproval took second place. The inscriptions seen on the Topkapı Saray group of prayer rugs are, admittedly, confined in each case to the upper part of the rug (framing bands, mihrab frame, spandrels or the apex of the mihrab arch), where the worshipper's feet should not tread anyway; but even for those of a less pietistic turn, the abundance of the inscriptions might seem to make the rugs hostages to fortune. It is highly probable, therefore, that they were not used for praying *on* at all, but were intended to be hung on the wall during prayers to serve as a mihrab. They would thus have been particularly appropriate for the women's quarters, for the women would have had no opportunity of going to the mosque and orthodox opinion encouraged women, anyway, to pray in the privacy of the home. If the

rugs were indeed meant for hanging, this would explain why they are mostly still in such good condition and, why, indeed, there are not more, or fewer, examples known: there are certainly too many such rugs in existence to make it plausible to argue that those in the Topkapı Saray were prayer rugs for the Sultans or even for their immediate families. None of them appear to bear signatures or dates, but some have been reported to bear verse inscriptions on the flat-woven band between pile and fringe. It would be desirable to have these published.

The scripts

As far as the actual rounded scripts are concerned, they range all the way from grandly drawn and arranged display scripts for the Āyat al-Kursī (Koran II, 255) in the principal border, somewhat reminiscent of architectural *thuluth*, though they are in general too slender and laxly written to ape the tile-mosaic inscriptions of the sixteenth–seventeenth centuries from Persia which are their closest analogues; via solid, workmanlike, *naskhī* for outer and inner borders (cf. *No. 6*) and carefully written and pointed 'Names of God' in the spandrels of mihrabs; to what should perhaps best be described as scribble, for the arches of mihrabs. Of these scripts only those used for the Names of God approximate at all closely to book hands, and although their arrangement is often peculiar, following a clockwise movement from the apex of the mihrab (with the result that most of them are viewed upside down), they show considerable regularity and vary far less than the hands used for borders. This regularity is perhaps all the more striking in that, as has already been observed, the inscriptions had to be redrawn practically every time they were used, in order to fit a different space.

The *naskhī* hands, both in the borders (see, for example, *Nos. 7* and *9*) and in the panels of *du'a* at the head of the mihrab niche (see, for example, *Nos. 6* and *25*), are most clearly paralleled on tombstones, not unnaturally, since tombstones, which are usually oriented in one way or another toward Mecca, are often decorated as mihrabs. By the late eighteenth century most of the tombstones in the Istanbul cemeteries featured the use of *nasta'līq*, but there had been an Anatolian tradition, from the Seljuk period onwards, of using strong plain *naskhī* for funerary inscriptions, and some of the inscriptions on the Topkapı Saray prayer carpets are close, for example, to those dating from the thirteenth–fourteenth centuries in the cemeteries of Ahlat, on Lake Van.[3] There is no need, of course, to go so far to find parallels, since forms of plain *naskhī* for funerary inscriptions persisted even in Istanbul into the twentieth century; but the source of the *naskhī* scripts would appear to be Anatolia rather than Iran.

Some of the rounded scripts, like the spidery straggling border seen in *No. 12* of the present volume, are bizarrely inappropriate, and their artlessness suggests the work of an unskilled craftsman, not a calligrapher at all. The characters are more or less well formed, but the failure to keep to a base line, which also shows itself in the main inscription band of the Āyat al-Kursī on the same piece, with its displeasing alternation of emptiness and crowding, represents an amateurish attempt to separate out an inscription from an over-elaborate scroll border or ground (compare *Nos. 7* and *9*) or to stretch an inscription designed as discrete cartouches into a continuous text.

This example is by no means the only case in which we might properly speak of incompetence, evidence of which to such a degree in a *Court* workshop might seem curious; and it is difficult to reconstruct the circumstances in which the piece might have reached the finished state – it may be related to the appearance on the inner inscription band and on the mihrab arch of Koranic inscriptions written in something like Persian *nasta‘līq* (in Turkish *ta‘līk*, confusingly, since the classical *ta‘līq*, a Chancery hand, is quite different in appearance). The term is not entirely apt, since the inscriptions are enclosed within cartouches (see, for example, *No. 17*) and are obliged to behave as if they were in a rounded script in which the presence of a horizontal base line can always be felt, but many of the letter forms and ligatures are characteristic of the *nasta‘līq* hand. *Nasta‘līq* was evolved in the late fourteenth and early fifteenth centuries in Royal scriptoria in Baghdad, Tabriz and Shiraz, and slightly later in Herat, as a literary script, i.e. not for Chancery use or for the Koran, although in later centuries in the Iranian world (Persia, Central Asia and Mughal India) it came to predominate, and although the famous sixteenth-century Safavid calligrapher, Shāh Maḥmūd al-Naysābūrī from Nishapur, wrote a Koran in *nasta‘līq* (Topkapı Saray Library, H.S.25; dated 945/1538–9 and illuminated in 970/1562–3 by Ḥasan al-Baghdādī, the chief illuminator of the studio of the Safavid Shah Ṭahmāsp), and may well have had some imitators, even in the eighteenth and nineteenth centuries it was rare for Korans to be written in *nasta‘līq*. The same is broadly true for Ottoman Turkey where, however, Koranic inscriptions in *nasta‘līq* are quite frequent on tombstones of the later period.

The reasons for the rarity of Korans written in *nasta‘līq* (the use of which, evidently, was never so disapproved of that it was prohibited) are not easy to ascertain, but it may be that the tendency of *nasta‘līq* hands to iron out the teeth of individual letters, making it correspondingly difficult to deduce which are the letters to which the pointing and dotting relates and which could conceivably have been felt to encourage misreadings or textual corruptions, may have dissuaded calligraphers who copied the Koran as a pious exercise from using it, for it would certainly have been considered impious to have misled the faithful by encouraging misreadings. Be that as it may, on a number of the Topkapı Saray rugs *nasta‘līq*, or something close to it, is used, not only for inscriptions in Persian or in praise of the Shī‘ī Imams, but also for Koranic friezes (see, for example, *Nos. 13–17, 19, 22, 23–25* and *35*), evidently in deliberate contrast to the scripts used for the inscriptions on other bands. Not that these examples give any appearance of consistency, for one rug with invocations to the Shī‘ī Imams (*No. 33*) is entirely in elegant rounded scripts, while another (*No. 31*) with Persian inscriptions is in fine *naskhī*: there is thus no constant relationship between the language, the religious tendencies and the scripts of these rugs.

In conclusion, one may make a few remarks on the subject of other scripts used on these rugs. No piece is known with the characteristic pseudo-Kufic borders of early Anatolian carpets, nor are there inscriptions actually in Kufic, which in Anatolia was already practically obsolete as early as 1300. What do occur are panels filled with ‘square Kufic’, that is, repeating inscriptions based on names like Muḥammad, ‘Alī and Allāh (for example, the lower medallions seen in *No. 20*), or else short inscriptions, usually *du‘ā* or invocations, in which either the letters of the Arabic alphabet are distorted to give the appearance of repetition or phrases with repeating combinations of letters are chosen. These include the Sunnī *shahāda* (*Lā ilāh ilā’llāh, Muḥammad rasūl Allāh* /'There is no god but God, Muḥammad is the Prophet of God'); a combination of the first part of the *shahāda* – *lā ilāh ilā’llāh* – with *al-ḥamdu li’llāh* ('Praise to God'), *subḥāna’llāh* or *Allāh subḥānahu* ('Glory be to God') and *Allāhu Akbar* ('God is All-great'); and a Koranic citation very similar in force, the second half of Sura XXI, 87. Inscriptions of this type are, unsurprisingly, highly illegible, a fact which limited the content of such panels to the best-known prayers or Koranic verses (another example is the end of Sura XI, 88); they first appear widely in the art and architecture of Īl-Khānid Iran in the late-thirteenth and early-fourteenth centuries. Although such inscriptions never went entirely out of fashion, they are not at all characteristic of calligraphy or decoration in Turkey or Iran in the eighteenth or nineteenth centuries. Their use here must therefore be yet another deliberate archaism.

In considering the Islamic decorative arts, there is always a temptation to underestimate the capacities of skilled craftsmen to work freehand from often quite basic sketches, and in the present group of carpets (see, for example, *Nos. 23–25*) the weavers evidently resorted to visual copies for the arabesque filling of the mihrab niche. It is, however, generally conceded that for the weaving of inscriptions cartoons would have been necessary, not only to facilitate an already complicated operation, but also – particularly in the case of Koranic inscriptions – to guarantee the correctness of the text which, in addition to having the dots (*tashkīl*) correctly added, should also indicate the pointing of the vowels (*ḥaraka*), doubled letters and silences. This safeguard was prompted by the fear of the '*ulamā*' that the text might be corrupted (*taḥrīf*), and for similar reasons the lawyers and theologians tended to look askance at incomplete citations of Koranic verses.

It should be said that, judged by these orthodox criteria, by no means all the inscriptions are canonically satisfactory. *Ḥaraka* is not always fully indicated, even in the grandest Koranic inscriptions, practically invariably of Sura II, 255, the Āyat al-Kursī; and the use of Sura XXI, 87, but only the latter part of it, for some of the panels filled with square Kufic, some of them in mirror image too, would surely have aroused censure, if any of the '*ulamā*' had succeeded in reading them. Indeed, not only do the square Kufic inscriptions throw *ḥaraka* and *tashkīl* to the winds, but the letter forms are distorted to the point of illegibility, so that, quite probably, none of the faithful realized that the words were Koranic or even that the content consisted of inscriptions at all.

The use of cartoons is particularly obvious in the pairs of panels containing square Kufic inscriptions, one of which is often quite capriciously reversed (see, for example, *No. 18*): if there seem to be no cases where both of a pair are reversed or where the pairs have got mixed up, that may have resulted from luck rather than calculation. In the case of other inscriptions, re-use of a cartoon is sometimes more difficult to detect, since cartouches may have been extended or enlarged, thus altering the appearance of the inscription. But, for example, the arrangement and execution of the Āyat al-Kursī (Koran II, 255) on two of the group (*Nos. 7, 9*) are clearly identical; while the rather spidery inscription seen on *No. 18*, in which some of the florets from the scroll background of these cartouches appear in black as meaningless *tashkīl*, is clearly a tracing, or something similar, from the cartoons used for the other two (*Nos. 7, 9*). Similarly, whereas the same cartoon appears to have been used for the Āyat al-Kursī in *Nos. 24* and *25*, in another case (*No. 23*) a tracing from it may have been adapted to cope with cartouches of different sizes.

On the other hand, some striking similarities exist (e.g., between *Nos. 8* and *34*), and these clearly are the result of skilful redrawing. The design of *No. 8*, which may well have been an experiment, has been ordered in such a way that the text of the Āyat al-Kursī overruns the third cartouche and has had to be continued below it in much smaller script – a feat which argues, in fact, for careful supervision of the designer himself. This feature may well have been seen as an inelegance, though it occurs so frequently in Arabic epigraphy that the calligrapher can scarcely have thought of it as such: in the case of *No. 34* the inscription has been skilfully redrawn to iron out the irregularity. In another case, on the other hand (*No. 13*), the Āyat al-Kursī appears to overrun its borders at the upper corners, possibly because of the use of cartoons too large for the dimensions of the carpet required, for the inner inscription (Sura XVII, 78–9) has run into similar difficulties. Was this an experiment with a new cartoon, or unintelligent copying of an earlier model? A second example (*No. 14*), in fact, appears to have been based on the same cartoon, or a shaky tracing from it, but marginally more successfully, though here too the use of cartouches to frame the three sections of the inscription would have made it less obvious that the draughtsman had no idea of how to turn a corner. The design seen in *No. 12* is similarly inept and shaky, but although its letter forms are broadly similar, it has been divided up very differently, perhaps in an attempt to avoid the messy effect of *No. 13*. Similar letter forms also appear in *Nos. 15* and *16*, redrawn but with a desperately crowded final cartouche, suggesting that the same cartoon had been redrawn in part: the outer and the inner inscriptions, which are both in Persian, are also markedly similar in appearance. Finally, but much more evenly, there are versions of the same cartoon in *Nos. 23–25* and in *No. 35*. Why this particular design, which begins elegantly enough but tends to end in disarray, should have gone through so many drafts is obscure, for the ordering and execution of the Āyat al-Kursī elsewhere (*Nos. 8* and *25* and *Nos. 7, 9* and *18*) provides a very much finer and more assured model.

Though the resemblances and groupings here relate only to the Āyat al-Kursī, and though the bands of inscription flanking it may be different both in content and disposition and in script, the rugs with Shī'ī inscriptions tend to be much more homogeneous in appearance. Thus, *Nos. 10* and *17*, with the Āyat al-Kursī in a sort of bold *nasta'līq*, bear identically written outer bands and an inner band with invocations to the Fourteen Immaculates. Not only that, but the inscriptions framing the mihrab arch and the filling of the spandrels with a selection of the '99 Names of God' are all identical in both script and disposition. The only difference is that the upper and lower pairs of cartouches of square Kufic have been transposed: their dimensions look different, but that is because there is less space in the corners, so that, in order to fit in, the inscriptions on *No. 17* have had to be cropped of some of their letters. Less similar, however, are *Nos. 20* and *34*, which nevertheless share a basic idea, namely a bold panel with the Shī'ī *shahāda* at the head of the carpet, flanked by the Āyat al-Kursī and an invocation to the Fourteen Immaculates. The rather exceptional use of the Āyat al-Kursī on the outer band of *No. 20* has made it necessary to include the next verse (II, 256) as well, to fill up the extra space. In the case of *No. 35*, where the Āyat al-Kursī appears, in contrast, on the inner band, the text has had to be crammed in and is particularly crowded towards the end. The two pieces are plainly related and in their different ways aim at a grand effect, but the solutions are rather different, making it difficult to suggest which, if any, was the original and which the adaptation.

Much the same applies to the flanking bands. For example, whereas both inner and outer bands on *Nos. 7* and *9* are identical, *No. 8* – which is very similar in general appearance – has an identical inner inscription, but its outer inscription – which is basically the same Koranic verses (XXVII, 30, and VI, 83) – has, doubtless for pietistic reasons, in place of the part of VI, 84 which follows on *Nos. 7* and *9*, prayers and invocations (*du'ā*), and has been redrawn entirely, though written in similar script. As for *No. 2*, where the flanking inscriptions are identical in content to both *Nos. 7* and *9* and are even in very similar scripts, each of them has been redrawn.

This comparison is not to exhaust the similarities in content, ordering and script of the inscriptions on the various pieces in the Topkapı Saray collections. The pieces show, however, that although the Koranic quotations they bear are from a limited group of verses, considerable variation is evident in their execution: the only cartoons which have been regularly re-used are those of square Kufic inscriptions when such are present. Otherwise, the pieces may show combinations of cartoons which do not imply any particular aim. They may, alternatively, be redrawn, sometimes, possibly, by reworking a tracing, but on other occasions so radically that they must have entailed a return to the drawing board. This is particularly the case with the selections of the '99 Names of God' used as the filling for the spandrels of mihrabs which, because of the lack of standardization of the dimensions and profiles of the mihrab niches, must have been redrawn in practically every case.

From these incessant reworkings we can draw a number of significant conclusions. First, the carpet workshop was under close supervision, with a staff of calligraphers in attendance to redraw or rework any inscriptions which had not given entirely satisfactory results, or to adapt them to spaces of different proportions: though one cannot be certain, the probability is that the cartoons would have been full size. It is difficult to calculate how many calligraphers there would have been, since although some of the scripts exhibit such peculiarities that one is inclined to see these characteristics as the work of a single hand, and since some of the apparent differences may be attributable to the knotting or to the sureness of the weavers' hands, the designs could well be the work of several pupils trained by a single master or of calligraphers adopting a 'house style'. *Nasta'līq* and the rounded hands, moreover, need not have been the work of different calligraphers, for in the later Ottoman Empire any competent and fully trained calligrapher would have been required to master both, and other scripts as well. But it is also very probable that the weavers themselves would have been capable of making minor adjustments or that minor redrawing of the cartoons, their mechanical reproduction by tracing, etc. could have been left to the head of the workshop.

The presence of cartoons and resident calligraphers may also suggest that there were designers attached to the workshop, or at least designs available which, in the case of elaborate counterpoints of spiral scrolls, cloudbands and palmettes, could have been worked up by the craftsmen freehand or reproduced by means of further cartoons and the effects achieved by judicious combination or compilation. Such could have been the stock in trade of any well-organized carpet workshop. But although designs recur and pairs of carpets may have been made (cf. *Nos. 7* and *9* and a piece from the Fletcher collection in the Metropolitan Museum of Art, New York), the degree of compilation, and of variation upon certain designs, is remarkable: for the most part, as few designs as inscriptions are exactly repeated, nor is there any regular correspondence between the choice of inscriptions, the hands they exhibit, the border scroll designs and the fillings of the field. The small number of known prayer carpets of this type and their concentration in the Topkapı Saray are enough to show that they were not mass-produced, but this considerable variation in the cartoons used, suggesting that the choice was left to the weavers, also indicates that the individual carpets were essentially occasional commissions. Thus, though their chronology is so far impossible to establish, they must mostly have been made one at a time, or at most in pairs, when the weavers no longer had before them a finished prototype to copy exactly. That then prompts the question as to what the weavers did between commissions and whether they might, instead of being members of a Court workshop, have been a commercial firm which, on request or command, undertook work for the Court. But, so far, there is nothing in the way of an answer.

Decoration

In decoration, the group of prayer rugs with a panel of *du'ā* placed at the head of the mihrab niche, though using more sophisticated colour contrasts and sharply drawn motifs (for example, *No. 2*), are indebted to carpet designs, notably those of the large medallion Uşaks which are primarily associated with the sixteenth century but which continued in production into the eighteenth century, and also, in layout and motifs, to prayer rugs associated with Uşak and Bergama in the eighteenth century and, in general, to the group of 'Transylvanian' prayer rugs (cf. *Nos. 2, 3, 5, 26*). More exceptionally, the fields of some rugs are reminiscent of the Anatolian 'Lotto' carpets (cf. *Nos. 4, 28, 30*) with their palmette motifs. If one were to seek prototypes of the decorative motifs of this group outside carpet-weaving, then the heavily imbricated cloud-scrolls and the bichrome split palmettes find similar treatment in Iznik tilework of the late-sixteenth century, where the foliate motifs often show decided modelling, and it may be that imitations or copies of these made at the Tekfur Sarayı potteries in Istanbul in the late-seventeenth and the eighteenth centuries contributed in some degree to keeping these motifs in circulation.

There are a number of hybrid or transitional pieces in the Topkapı Saray collections which may suggest that this group and the more elaborate inscription rugs are from the same looms, notably the inscription rugs with fawn grounds on which spiral scrollwork is overlaid with heavy cloud-bands and other motifs: thus *No. 3* is decidedly similar in treatment to the elaborate inscription rug, *No. 33*, with its subdued three-colour decoration in black, white and fawn. However, in this latter group, though some of the decorative motifs seen in isolation may recall the decoration of a series of sixteenth-century Kashan or Tabriz carpets,[4] neither their drawing nor their arrangement is characteristic of carpet design; on the other hand, it strongly suggests the arts of the book, notably illumination and the decoration of bindings. The resemblances are legion. Thus, while the filling of mihrab spandrels with polychrome scale-like compartments (cf., for example, *Nos. 10–12, 17, 19*) may remotely suggest a derivation

from the doublures of sixteenth-century Safavid bindings with their panels of contrasting colours, the filling of the mihrab niche of *No. 34*, with its decorative contours, directly recalls such panelled doublures, and the overlay of scrolls or arabesques is a reminiscence of the filigree work which traditionally accompanies such panelling. It is worth remark, moreover, that the repertoire of rich stylized chinoiserie peony- and lotus-scroll with cloud-bands (compare the spandrels of *Nos. 23–25*) was by 1550 fully established in Ottoman binding, not merely in Safavid Iran, and that, evidently because the stamps continued in use, it persists into the eighteenth century or even beyond.

This decorative repertoire underwent a striking revival in the early eighteenth century in lacquerwork associated with the school of Edirne (*Edirnekārī*), both for mirror-cases and small portable objects, and also for bindings. It is characterized by medallions with spiralling blossom-scrolls and cloud-bands set on dense fields of peony- or lotus-scroll, feathery leaves and cloud-bands. There is in the Topkapı Saray Library a famous binding of the verse of Sultan Aḥmed III (A.3652), dated 1136/1723–4 and signed by the craftsman 'Alī Üsküdārī.[5] This binding may well be seen as a worked-up version of the carpet-field designs seen in *Nos. 18* and *35* and – if that be conceded – there is an even closer parallel between a lacquer binding of 1795 (Topkapı Saray Library, E.H.1682)[6] and another carpet illustrated in the present volume (*No. 32*), with scrollwork of peonies, lotuses and feathery leaves. This is, of course, not to argue that lacquer bindings, whether contemporary or of relatively recent date, were actually the source for the decoration of the Topkapı Saray carpets, but merely to show that the classical repertoire of Ottoman illuminated decoration had survived, or been revived, well beyond the sixteenth century.

In fact the carpet designs are clearly indebted to illumination, either as the common source of the binding designs and scrollwork, or as an additional source for highly eclectic designers who were also bookworms. The rather complex and confused borders of several carpets (*Nos. 7, 9, 10, 22* for example), with a ground of spiral scrolls overlaid by split palmettes, sharply drawn and almost modelled, through which wriggle cloud-bands which are not always well differentiated in colour, is a moderately effective version of a device frequently employed in illumination. Another characteristic illumination border is the notched stems and foliate heads with scroll filling and ground used to good effect in, for example, *No. 16*. These motifs are also frequent in sixteenth-century Ottoman illumination, though they may well have been taken over from contemporary Safavid illumination executed at Tabriz;

and if in other features as well these carpets are somewhat reminiscent of the great sixteenth-century carpets of Tabriz and Kashan, that must be because the Persian types also are strongly indebted to illumination and may well have had their patterns drawn by designers who had been trained as illuminators in the Safavid scriptorium. The common vocabulary of ornament in sixteenth-century Turkey and Iran makes it unfruitful to consider whether the designs are more 'Persian' than 'Ottoman', but it makes it less surprising that earlier authorities like Sarre were tempted to attribute the Topkapı Saray prayer rugs, doubtless, however, by elimination, to sixteenth-century Kashan or Tabriz.

Given the presence of such eclectic carpet designers at the Ottoman Court, it would be rather surprising not to find further influence from Iznik tilework, in particular from the great tile mihrabs of the mosques of Istanbul dating from the later sixteenth century, which were accessible to all. Indeed, the flowering Prunus trees with cypresses flanking a vase containing a wreath-like floral bouquet (on *Nos. 7, 9*, etc.) may derive ultimately from compositions of flowering Prunus decorating the mausoleum of Hurrem Sultan (died 1558) at Süleymaniye or the porch of the mosque of Rüstem Paşa (died 1561), though at some distance and with suggestions of early-seventeenth-century tilework, like that of the mosque of Sultan Aḥmed; other uses of these motifs in carpets (cf. *Nos. 10, 11*) are more stylized and were evidently worked up by the weavers themselves at the loom. Tilework, for example from the mosque of Sokollu Meḥmed Paşa (inaugurated 1571), may also have inspired the medallions which fill some of the niches (for example, *Nos. 12, 21*). It is, however, rather striking how the carpet medallions came to resemble fat vases, hanging ornaments or lamps (particularly *No. 34*), or even the Sufi head-dress (*tāc*) which is illustrated in late Ottoman works of Bektaşi Sufi piety.

Almost certainly the vase, which on *No. 21* appears as the base of a medallion, was the original idea, and the 'tray' on which the vases on *Nos. 7* and *9* stand, like the bouquets they hold, were metamorphosed into types of foliate medallion. At an early stage in the evolution of the motif (*No. 16*), however, the vase acquires crowns, around the neck, at the base and even, inverted, as a stand, with chinoiserie lotus- or peony-heads playing an important part in the decorative scheme. This, and the numerous variations upon it, has little to do with tilework, and the conspicuous use of the crown motif recalls rather Bursa silks of the sixteenth and seventeenth centuries, almost certainly after Venetian prototypes which combine Ottoman motifs with conspicuous crowns. It should be noted in passing that the carpets

show otherwise no obvious indebtedness to textiles of any culture or period.

The vase-medallions when transmuted into hanging lamps – with the conspicuous exception of that seen in *No. 33*, with its three hanging vases, and of the single vase of *No. 32* – have, however, little resemblance either to a vase or to a mosque lamp. That of *No. 34*, the most accomplished, with its crowned neck and the inverted crown at its base, has three large dependent tassels and may be a conscious reminiscence of the jewelled gold pendants made for the Sultans to hang over their thrones or to be offered to the Ka'ba at Mecca or to the shrine at Medina. As for the medallion-vase of *No. 14*, with stylized floral chains and what looks like a portfolio above the vase, the design has become bizarrely confused.

To adduce further resemblances would be easy but might lead to an unwelcome impression of floundering, rather than conveying the evident eclecticism in the choice of motifs. Though some carpets of the group are plainly versions of others, without recourse to a new design, pieces like *Nos. 7, 9, 18, 32* and *34* are not versions of known carpets at all, or of other textiles, and their designs have been compiled from disparate sources. The most important were adopted from illumination – panelled borders with scrolling ornament overlaid by split palmettes or cloud-bands; inscription cartouches; and complex scrollwork of feathery leaves and stylized chinoiserie peony- and lotus-scroll. All these motifs remained popular in varying degrees in eighteenth-century Ottoman Turkey, either through adaptation or through re-use of sixteenth-century bookbinders' stamps or other patterns, or through revivals in classical Ottoman ornament like the *Edirnekārī* lacquerwork. The ultimate effect is, of course, so different that, as in the case of the borders, vase and scroll ground of *No. 19*, it is difficult to avoid the impression that the designer turned back to sixteenth-century illumination for his models, which would have implied having access to the Topkapı Saray library. And that is worth remark, even if we cannot guess when the designer might have lived or what his circumstances may have been: for in Islam, and particularly in Ottoman and Safavid art, such rampant eclecticism is exceptional.

In the absence of an independent chronology and fixed dates for the manufacture of these prayer rugs, or of an idea of the position and status of the craftsmen or even of the patrons for whom they worked, it is impossible to say more. For, paradoxically, our knowledge of the Ottoman decorative arts becomes progressively less as the eighteenth and nineteenth centuries advance: the rise of Ottoman 'Baroque' and the increasing impact of Westernizing influence, moreover, make a return to the classical themes of Ottoman illumination very difficult to place. It is not even clear that in the nineteenth century Ottoman Turkey underwent the passion for revivalism which swept Europe, or that it took the form of a return to traditional preoccupations rather than, for example, an interest in Gothic revival, for which there is evidence in the architecture of Istanbul in the later nineteenth century. W. B. Denny,[7] concluding that the Topkapı Saray inscription rugs must be dated almost at the end of the nineteenth century, has suggested that the designs may be associated with pan-Islamic movements in the last period of the Ottoman Caliphate or with a nostalgic return to Seljuk and early Ottoman roots in Anatolia which shows itself in the writings of Ottoman historians in the early twentieth century. Almost certainly, however, the rugs had all been made by the time such ideas became fashionable; nor is there much evidence that their designs had any effect upon the decorative arts.

So far, the prevailing view that these Palace carpets are not of any great antiquity but are historicizing pieces to be dated to the nineteenth or, at the very earliest, the late-eighteenth century, has been taken for granted. Since, however, there is no available documentary evidence for the existence or operation of a Palace workshop in this late period, it is necessary to reconsider the views of the classical writers on these carpets, F. R. Martin, Friedrich Sarre and Hermann Trenkwald, who, with varying degrees of hesitation, concluded that the carpets were of some antiquity, and of the late Kurt Erdmann, who concluded with less hesitation that they were not. Though none of their conclusions are entirely convincing, their reasons for asserting them are of lasting interest.

Provenance

The first traceable carpet of this inscription group to attract attention in Europe is a piece acquired by the Parisian collector, Albert Goupil, published in 1885,[8] and having a design which probably is closest to *No. 25* in the present volume. Goupil's taste was particularly for Mamlūk inlaid metalwork and enamelled glass (which he was notorious for 'improving', notably by adding silver inlay to pieces he considered insufficiently decorative). How he acquired the carpet is not recorded, but its illustration by Henri Lavoix in the *Gazette des Beaux-Arts*, along with Mamlūk antiquities, suggests both that Goupil admired it and that it was thought at the time to be of some antiquity. This carpet, or its double, seems to have passed into the Paravicini collection.[9]

F. R. Martin, whose *A History of Oriental Carpets before 1800* (Vienna 1908) was an early attempt to systematize the historical evidence for carpets in the Middle East (though many of his attributions have since been superseded or rejected), published two carpets of this type. The first of these[10] is heavily brocaded with silver or gold thread and the spandrels are filled with selections from the '99 Names of God', but curiously arranged within sausage-like bladders. The field of the niche is somewhat similar to that of *No. 18* in the present volume, and the main scroll border is practically identical to that of the Fletcher carpet in the Metropolitan Museum of Art, New York. Martin states that the carpet came from somewhere near Istanbul, and attributes it possibly to Amul, *c.*1550, though he adds, confusingly, that he had 'a certain impression that it is to be connected closely with carpets made by the Turcomans between the Persian frontier and Bukhara'. It was included in the great exhibition of Islamic art held in Munich in 1910,[11] later being published by Arthur Upham Pope[12] with a slightly hesitant attribution to sixteenth-century Tabriz; at this point the piece was in the Bacri collection. Martin's second specimen (Fig. 147), in the Musée Historique de Tissus, Lyons, was attributed by him to Yazd, *c.*1550. This is a prayer rug with the Ka'ba represented at the head of the mihrab niche. The border is of rosettes and foliate panels with small transverse cartouches, some of which bear *nasta'līq* inscriptions which remain unread. The idea and realization of the border are very similar to the Yerkes medallion carpet, also published by Pope,[13] which is now generally agreed to be one of the same group (see below). This piece does not appear to have been known to Martin but, significantly, he associates the Lyons rug with a rectangular carpet 'of bad design' with panels of *nasta'līq* and a field of busily wriggling spiral arabesques which was sold in Paris in 1907 and bought by 'Alī Ibrāhīm Pasha, whose important collection of carpets is now in the Museum of Islamic Art in Cairo. The latter carpet is now generally agreed not to be of sixteenth-century date but, for what it is worth, Martin states that it came from the Cathedral of Palanza in Spain.

The Munich exhibition also included a carpet from this group, then in the Imperial Ottoman Museum (that is, the precursor of the present Türk ve Islâm Eserleri Müzesi in Istanbul), reported to be from the tomb of Selīm I (1512–20), with a panel of *du'ā* above the mihrab niche, cloud-band spandrels and a niche filled with thin symmetrical arabesques which seem to be a version of the fatter arabesques seen on *No. 19* in the present volume: this example was attributed to 'Anatolia, sixteenth-century'. No-one ever appears to have enquired how many carpets of this group might still be in the collections of the Türk ve Islâm Eserleri Müzesi.

The next occasion on which any prayer carpets of this group appear to have been considered is the still standard work by Friedrich Sarre and Hermann Trenkwald, *Alt-orientalische Teppiche*.[14] They published two carpets from the Metropolitan Museum of Art, New York: that from the Fletcher collection (Volume II, Plate 51) is for all practical purposes identical to one in the Topkapı Saray (cf. *No. 18*), though very slightly shorter and having a cotton rather than a woollen warp; the second (Volume II, Plate 52), from the Altman collection, was formerly in the possession of Stefano Bardini in Florence. The inscriptions on this carpet and their arrangement are identical to those on a piece in the Topkapı Saray (cf. *No. 20*), though the Altman carpet is slightly shorter, as well as markedly narrower, and the warp is likewise cotton, not wool. The field and the border designs, moreover, are somewhat different and suggest that the Metropolitan piece is a coarser copy, doubtless woven from cartoons traced from the originals.

If Sarre and Trenkwald felt any discomfort in attributing these pieces to sixteenth-century Iran, they do not express it. Arthur Upham Pope was, however, by no means convinced that the three pieces from the Topkapı Saray that he published in *Survey of Persian Art* (*Nos. 8, 9, 33* in the present volume) were Persian, but he provisionally attributed them to North-West Iran, possibly Tabriz in the early-seventeenth century. His basis for so doing appears to have been: their resemblance to 'a fragmentary carpet from the Ardabil mosque'; two comparable or similar carpets in the Ardabil treasury, which remain unpublished; and a report by the traveller Jean Baptiste Tavernier that in the late sixteenth century Shah 'Abbās possessed in Isfahan a carpet decorated only with inscriptions. This evidence may or may not be convincing.

Pope also published the Goupil–Paravicini–Yusuf Kamāl carpet, with its characteristically Safavid border of foliate heads and notched stems, which seems to be a finer version of the borders of *Nos. 16* and *19* in the present volume. A further piece, stated to be in the National Museum in Teheran (though it has not been on show there for many years now), is published with a similarly hesitant attribution (Plate 1168b). Could it in fact have been from Ardabil? The disposition of the Āyat al-Kursī lacks the square panels of square Kufic in the corners, and the scrolling border below is a counterpoint of thin cloud-scrolls and tied cloud-bands: it has no parallel in any other carpet of this group so far published. The filling of the mihrab niche is a medallion placed on an inverted crown, as on *Nos. 12* and *22* in the

present volume, though filled with a denser lotus-scroll. The field is probably closest to *No. 12*, though the choice of inscriptions is different.

With these carpets Pope also published the Yerkes carpet, a silk medallion and arabesque piece brocaded with metal thread, with a similar attribution; it bears a narrow guard-band with panels of *nasta'līq* inscription and a main border of rosettes and foliate cartouches with small transverse bars, most of them with further *nasta'līq* inscriptions, which remain unread. The decorative style has something in common with *No. 2* in the present volume. Finally, he included a triple prayer rug from the Rabénou collection (Plate 1171), with split-palmette scrolls close to those on *Nos. 23–25* in the present volume and with the lower part of the niches filled with a double foliate or floral scrollwork, somewhat reminiscent of *No. 19*. Few of the Topkapı Saray pieces, however, have as few cloud-scrolls or cloud-bands as this.

With the more critical attitude of the post-war decades to the contribution of Iran in general and of the Persian carpet in particular to the arts of Islam, and with the increasing scholarly objections to the work of Martin and to the *Survey of Persian Art*, Pope's doubtless insufficiently hesitant attributions came under fire. The eclecticism, the brilliant, even gaudy, colours of the carpets and their often strikingly good condition led Kurt Erdmann to the obvious conclusion that the carpets were not old at all and that they were in fact products of the nineteenth-century looms of Hereke.[15] These were set up in 1843 by Sultan 'Abdü'l-Mecīd and, at least on the basis of orders executed in the twentieth century, have become closely associated with the manufacture of historicizing carpets. An example of such carpets is possibly a piece now in the Vakıflar Carpet Museum at Sultanahmet in Istanbul (No. 140), from the Muṣṭafā Ağa Camii (a late-nineteenth-century mosque near the railway station at Sirkeci in Istanbul). With the group Erdmann also associated a number of medallion carpets with inscriptions, mostly in Persian and in *nasta'līq*, including the 'Salting' carpet in the Victoria and Albert Museum, London, which was first published in 1883.[16]

It has recently come to be agreed, however, that Erdmann's attribution to Hereke is not entirely satisfactory, at least for the group as a whole, for the Hereke factory was originally established not for carpet-weaving at all, but to make silk and cotton fabrics for the Ottoman Court: in 1850 a hundred jacquard looms were added and the cotton looms were moved to create a cotton-weaving factory at Bakırköy, near Istanbul. The first evidence for carpet manufacture at Hereke, moreover, seems to occur in 1891, when carpet looms were established there, worked by craftsmen from

Gördes and Demirci. Details about the early production the Hereke looms in the nineteenth century are extremely hard to come by, and it may be that the looms set up in 1891 were not the first carpet looms there; however, this late date makes carpets like the one in the Goupil collection difficult to account for. For that reason, as well as for others, it has recently been suggested that the carpets were woven at Feshane,[17] near Eyüp at the head of the Golden Horn, where a state factory, the Defterdar Mensucat Fabrikası, was founded in 1836 to make fezzes for the Ottoman army and civil service. This later turned to carpet-making and to the manufacture of heavy woollen cloth. Manufacture in or near Istanbul is certainly consistent with the present location or known provenance of most carpets of the group, including the carpet in the National Museum in Teheran published by Pope, which could well have been a royal gift to a Qajar ruler or prince. But if Feshane was the factory, how was it that carpets of this type were not woven for a much larger market? Further investigation of the question is much hampered by the general state of ignorance on the industrialization of nineteenth-century Istanbul.

Though we have little choice but to accept it, a mid-nineteenth-century dating for the group, or the earliest of them, is not entirely satisfactory, since it involves the total rejection of the views of Martin and Sarre, who were connoisseurs as well as scholars, not only of Islamic art in general but of textiles in particular. The history of carpet attributions has, admittedly been more remarkable for wild imagination than for common sense, but it scarcely bears belief that scholars who in so many ways contributed so much to our knowledge of the carpet-making tradition in Islam should have been so blinded by appearances that they failed to realize that the carpets before them were no more than fifty years old, if that. At the time they wrote, these carpets must have looked fairly old, which suggests that even before the Feshane factory was established there were looms producing them.

One of the most interesting carpets of the group is a neglected example, which is admittedly no beauty, published by Sarre and Trenkwald,[18] which they report to have been found in a mosque in Aleppo. It is a rectangular inscription rug, measuring 265 × 165 cm, having a curious irregular cruciform medallion in the field with part of a similar medallion below and *Allāhu akbar kabīran*/'God is All-great, greatly' at the tip of each arm. Its condition is very poor and it is accordingly difficult to tell whether cloud-bands on the upper border or rather haphazard squares of lotus-scroll at the corners are repairs or not. The rest of the border inscription has been read as the Āyat al-Kursī, though

the sides bear panels, some of them containing a repeating formula. There are two pairs of panels of square Kufic, all bearing the latter part of Koran XXI, 87: the upper pair are reversed. The ground is divided horizontally into strips or bands which are then irregularly divided into compartments with selections of the '99 Names of God' in the form of invocations, some of them possibly in reverse.

The ineptness of the design, the doddery script, the dreary colours (a dull-red border and a dun-coloured field with very few colour accents) are all a clear indication that the rug is a copy, at several removes, of an inscription carpet of the Topkapı Saray group, though not a prayer rug. How much of a chronological gap such a copy might imply, or whether it was an indication of a degree of production for the mass market – numerous poorer imitations circulating simultaneously with the Court prototypes – is impossible to say. However, the miserably worn condition of this piece by the time it came on the European market is an indication of sorts that it was not of nineteenth-century date but at least slightly older. If so, it must have been made somewhere other than at Feshane.

Beyond this conclusion, however, there is irritatingly little we can now do to localize the place of manufacture of the presumed prototypes of the Topkapı Saray group. For although the carpets fall broadly into two groups (those with a panel of *du'ā* above the mihrab niche having an appearance somewhat reminiscent of eighteenth-century Uşak or Bergama designs; and those which are characterized by multiple inscription bands), it is still premature to claim that they exhibit sufficient technical differences to suggest that they must have been the products of different factories – or, conceivably, of the same factory at different periods in its existence. Anyway, even within one group the materials and specifications of the warp, the weft and the pile are very variable. The presence, on some examples of each group, of inscriptions in Persian may be significant, though it can scarcely localize production, and, in any case, the occurrence of inscriptions which are Shī'ī in tenor is no evidence that any of the carpets were made in Iran. Ottoman Turkey housed a considerable Shī'ī and 'Alevi (Kızılbaş) population, and most Sunnīs would have been broad-minded enough to ignore the rather mild sectarian implications of the inscriptions. Moreover, knowledge of the Persian language was widespread in Turkey right up to the fall of the Ottoman Empire. And though, almost inevitably, some of the carpets include motifs which Ottoman Turkey employed in common with Safavid Iran in the sixteenth century, the eclectic choice of motifs would have been easier in Anatolia.

It is similarly difficult or impossible to separate out, within the group as it survives, a class of prototypes which could then have been imitated, perhaps as late as the end of the nineteenth century. Two documents which have sometimes been cited as evidence for the manufacture of such prototypes turn out on inspection to be of little relevance. One of these is an order dated 4 Muḥarram 1019/30 March 1610 to the kadis of the *sancak* of Kütahya[19] prohibiting carpets made there henceforth from bearing either inscriptions or depictions of the Ka'ba. There is no reason, however, to identify the banned carpets with any of the Topkapı Saray group, and it is apparent from the context that the reason for the edict was partly that carpets bearing Koranic inscriptions or a depiction of the Ka'ba were frowned upon by the authorities anyway, but also because they were being bought by infidels (*kefere taifesi*) and by merchants (*tüccār taifesi*). Prayer rugs with such designs thus risked defilement, from the feet of Christians and foreigners, and the authorities were therefore attempting to control the design of carpets made for export, if not to forbid carpet exports altogether. None of the Topkapı Saray group can be shown to have been exported.

The second document,[20] dated Rabī' I 1139/November 1726, is an order to the kadi of Uşak to the effect that, since carpets ordered for the Hırka-i Saadet apartments in the Topkapı Saray were not ready, work was to be concentrated upon them, except for carpets destined for Egypt or for the trade. Its force is not entirely clear, and it may be that the clerk had misunderstood it, for it would be more reasonable to assume that the kadi should have recourse to Egypt and the trade (at his own expense) in order to supply the carpets which had been ordered. The mention of the Hırka-i Saadet apartments, however, has suggested that the Topkapı Saray carpets were in fact woven for the purpose, or for the staff of the Has Oda (Privy Chamber), forty in all, who were in attendance upon the Hırka-i Saadet apartments and the mantle of the Prophet. However, since the point of the order is that the required carpets had not been finished, it cannot tell us much about what they were.

The role of centralized demand or of Court taste in the Ottoman carpet industry is, in the light of the documents and of the extant material, rather difficult to assess. In the sixteenth century, doubtless, as with the Chinese porcelains which came to the Topkapı Saray, the almost uninterrupted flow of booty and tribute may have made the authorities content to accept passively whatever carpets came their way. Later in the century, there was indeed a revolution in Court taste, in favour of the 'Court' carpets which are now generally agreed to

have been woven in Cairo to designs sent from Istanbul. To judge from the extant examples, the number of basic patterns was small but there were very considerable variations upon them – in materials as well as in treatment of decorative motifs – and for clients also well away from the Ottoman Court. There is, for example, a rug in the Textile Museum in Washington, D.C. (1967.24.1), formerly in the Benguiat collection, that is said to have come from 'a mosque in Spain', as well as the group of synagogue rugs or hangings in Cairene style. The Washington piece shows some similarities to that in the Topkapı Saray (cf. *No. 1*) and, like it, is somewhat exceptional in being all-wool.

The fineness and brilliant effect of these Cairene carpets leave no doubt that, for a time at least, they were the height of fashion. Yet, paradoxically, just as the craftsmen, the *ḳāliçebāfān-i Ḥāṣṣa*, on the Palace registers were about to be disbanded in the reign of Sultan Ahmed I, the dated and datable Cairene rugs show that Ottoman demand for them was decreasing; and although it is difficult to imagine that their manufacture entirely ceased after 1620 or so, we have absolutely no idea of what Ottoman rugs might have displaced them at the Court or where these might have been made. The Court carpets in the seventeenth century could conceivably not have been Ottoman at all, though it is scarcely plausible that the flow of Persian carpets into Istanbul in the seventeenth and eighteenth centuries was so vast that, once again, the authorities could afford passively to accept whatever Persian carpets became available by way of tribute and trade, rather than taking active steps to obtain particular favourites.

This absence of information makes the Palace carpets (*Nos. 2–35*) a particularly puzzling phenomenon. They are very different from the Europeanized designs of Hereke in the early twentieth century and from other finely woven Ottoman rugs of the period. Why are they found only in the Topkapı Saray collections and not in any of the new palaces built on the Bosphorus which were so much more popular with the Sultans as residences in the later nineteenth century? and why, moreover, are they, apart from the single Cairene carpet discussed above, the only Court carpets in the Topkapı Saray? It is, therefore, possible that they were specific commissions to fill a gap – perhaps created by the destruction of a large part of the Palace carpet store in one of the periodic fires which ravaged the Topkapı Saray and its outbuildings. Alternatively, their historicizing appearance, which is not in general characteristic of the decorative arts in the nineteenth century, may indicate that they were intended for a shrine, possibly the Hırka-i Saadet apartments in the Topkapı Saray in one of its later restorations.

NOTES TO CHAPTER 2

1   Martin Hinds and Hamdi Sakkout, *Arabic documents from the Ottoman period from Qaṣr Ibrim* (Egypt Exploration Society, London 1986).

2   Kurt Erdmann, 'Inscriptions on carpets' in *Seven Hundred Years of Oriental Carpets*, ed. Hanna Erdmann, trans. May H. Beattie and Hildegard Herzog (London 1970), 163–6; Yusuf Dural, 'Halı ve seccadelerdeki yazı süslemeleri', *Türkiyemiz* 17 (Istanbul 1975), 15.

3   J. M. Rogers, 'Calligraphy and common script: Epitaphs from the cemeteries of Aswan and Ahlat' in Priscilla P. Soucek (ed.), *Essays in Memory of Richard Ettinghausen* (New York University Press, New York 1987).

4   The conspicuous vases on some of the carpets (e.g. *Nos. 13, 15* and *20* in the present volume) seem to derive from a vase filled with confronted peacocks and flanked by pomegranate trees, but with curious dragon brackets below on lion or *qilin* feet instead of the characteristic inverted crown, on a multiple medallion and animal carpet in the Victoria and Albert Museum illustrated by Arthur Upham Pope in the *Survey of Persian Art* (Oxford 1939), Plate 1131, and attributed by him to Tabriz, early sixteenth century. There are, however, rather similar vases on the Baker carpet in the Metropolitan Museum of Art (*Survey of Persian Art*, Plate 1153), which is now accepted not to be of sixteenth-century date.

5   Kemal Çığ, *Türk kitap kapları* (Istanbul 1971), Plate 35; *The Anatolian Civilisations*, exhibition catalogue (Istanbul 1983), II, E316. It is difficult to explain this revival or even to trace its impact on basic decorative arts like illumination. But it may have influenced the arabesque decoration of some late Ottoman embroideries.

6   Çığ, op. cit., Plate 50.

7   Walter B. Denny, 'The origin and development of Ottoman Court carpets' in Robert Pinner and W. B. Denny (eds.) *Carpets of the Mediterranean countries 1400–1600* (= *Oriental Carpet and Textile Studies* II) (London 1986), 243–59.

8   Henri Lavoix, 'La collection Albert Goupil. II. L'art oriental', *Gazette des Beaux-Arts*, 2ᵉ période, XXXII (1885), 287–307.

9   Published as such by Pope in *Survey of Persian Art* (Oxford 1939), Plate 1165. It is also illustrated in Z. M. Ḥasan's, *Aṭlas al-funūn al-zukhrafiyya wa'l-taṣāwīr al-islāmiyya* (Cairo 1956), Fig. 662, the caption stating that it was then in the collection of Prince Yūsuf Kamāl. The carpet is therefore very probably still in Cairo.

10   Martin, op. cit., Fig. 132.

11   *Meisterwerke Muhammedanischer Kunst*, exhibition catalogue (Munich 1910–11), Plate 83, catalogue no. 61.

12   *Survey of Persian Art*, Plate 1166.

13   Ibid., Plate 1170a.

14   Friedrich Sarre and Hermann Trenkwald, *Alt-orientalische Teppiche* (Vienna-Leipzig 1926).

15   Kurt Erdmann, 'Persian carpets of Turkish provenance' in *Seven Hundred Years of Oriental Carpets* (op. cit., note 2), 76–80.

16   The others specifically mentioned are the Labanov-Rostovsky carpet (Hermitage); a carpet from the Czartoryski collection in Kraków; the Marquand carpet in the Philadelphia Museum of Art; the Baker carpet in the Metropolitan Museum of Art, New York; a carpet from the Goupil collection in the Musée Historique de Tissus, Lyons; the 'Alī Ibrāhīm Pasha carpet in the Museum of Islamic Art, Cairo (mentioned above); and 'one in the Topkapı Saray'. There may well be others, of course.

17   Ülkü Bilgin, '19 yüzyıl saray seccadeleri', *Sanat Dunyamız* 17 (September 1979), 18–21; W. B. Denny, art cit. (note 7). May H. Beattie, however, cautiously cites – in 'Hereke', *Halı* IV/2 (1981), 128–34 – an uncorroborated Turkish source to the effect that carpet-weaving at Hereke began in 1864; if this can be shown to have been the case, Hereke may come back into the picture.

18   Op. cit. (note 14), I, Plate 32.

19   Ahmet Refik, *Hicrî on birinci asırda Istanbul hayatı (1000–1100)* (Istanbul 1931), No. 83.

20   Ahmet Refik, *Hicrî onikinci asırda Istanbul hayatı (1100–1200)* (Istanbul 1930), No. 119.

3

Turkish carpets at home and abroad

APART from the flourishing export trade in the fifteenth–seventeenth centuries from Egypt and Anatolia to Italy and Northern Europe and to Transylvania (Siebenbürgen; Erdel) and the existence of numerous surviving rugs in churches and in museums in Turkey, Europe and the United States, there are two main sources for the history of early Ottoman carpets: Italian and, later, German, Dutch and Flemish painting,[1] where the works in which carpets are depicted are often precisely datable and give a vivid impression of the carpets' appearance but little indication of their provenance; and inventories, lists of tariffs and registers of fixed prices, which rarely convey any indication of the appearance of carpets but, even if they give rise to more problems than they solve, do give an idea of provenance, immediate if not remote. A typical problem of this sort is associated with the *cimiscasachi* carpets (evidently, from Çemişgezek on the Upper Euphrates) which, Marino Sanuto (who was secretary of the Venetian Council of Ten from *c*.1490 to 1533) records, were brought out to bedeck the Doge's Palace and the balconies overlooking St Mark's Square in Venice on great religious feasts or State occasions, and which may well be those represented in Giovanni Mansueti's contribution to the cycle of paintings depicting a miracle of the Holy Cross (Venice, Accademia), and may have continued to be used till the later sixteenth century.[2] Çemişgezek had no history as a carpet-manufacturing centre and in the late-fifteenth and early-sixteenth centuries was in the middle of territory violently disputed by the Ottomans and the growing power of Safavid Iran with its Kızılbaş forces: what therefore are we to make of the attribution? So often in the sixteenth–seventeenth centuries, lists of goods grouped by provenance fail to distinguish between styles or types, to which a place name may be applied to provide a trade term, and the actual place of acquisition; chance purchases made, say, in the bazaar at Çemişgezek may not have been pieces from that locality.

Nor are the numerous reports of European travellers of the sixteenth and seventeenth centuries necessarily of much more help, since, as luck would have it, few of them chanced to visit the great carpet-weaving centres of Anatolia in the old province of Germiyan, west of Kütahya. Travellers, moreover, must often have been fatigued or have relied on hearsay or unreliable or too obliging informants, or they may have failed to make detailed notes for fear of being accused of spying, or like the French ambassadors to Süleymān the Magnificent have been too grand to condescend to simple observation. This must explain why, for example, the great naturalist Pierre Belon du Mans, who travelled in Anatolia in the 1540s and whose work is full of the most useful observations, could, when it comes to carpet manufacture, give such a garbled account as the following:[3]

> Tous les tapiz coupez qu'on apporte de Turquie, sont seulement faits depuis la ville de Cogne [Konya] en Cilicie, uisques à Carachara [Gangra/Çankırı] ville de Paphlagonie. Nous avons dit que les fins chamelots [mohair] sont faits de poil de cheures à Angouri [Ankara], qui est la premiere ville à Cappadoce: & les tapiz sont aussi faits de poil de cheures mais ceux qu'on fait au Caire, ne sont guere beaux: car ils sont seulement tissuz en toille bigaree [striped?; or bicoloured cotton thread?]. Ceux de Adena [Adana] sont faicts en feutres, fort legers & mols, à se coucher dessus.

It is difficult to imagine how he could ignore the ubiquitous Anatolian kilims or the famous Cairene pile rugs or concentrate upon the production of mohair carpets at Ankara when the only references to mohair floor-coverings in the Ottoman documents show that these were felts and mostly from Salonike or the Balkans: but travel was arduous and often difficult, and information hard to obtain and evaluate.

Halil Inalcık has, however, pointed out[4] that although local types of carpet were by the eighteenth century made practically all over Anatolia, the most famous carpets of Ottoman times all came from centres in the old province of Germiyan in the basin of the upper Gediz river, which is both surrounded by mountains and traversed by fast-flowing streams – Uşak, Kula, Gördes, Demirci and Selendi. Adjacent were the famous alum mines of Gediz, on the southern skirt of the Şaphanedağ, while the Kula area was held to produce the best madder dye (*kökboya*). The nomadic Yürüks in the high pasture lands supplied wool and skilled labour, while the port of Izmir was a convenient centre for marketing and shipping carpets for export. The expansion of Izmir in the late-eighteenth and the nineteenth centuries, the constant pressure upon the Yürüks to become settled and the gradual transformation of carpet-weaving into a highly organized mass-production industry principally involved changes in scale, and it is probable that the basic market structure would have been present in its elements from the very first, that is, from the time Anatolian carpets first attracted the attention of the Ottoman authorities. Given the ease of transporting craftsmen, looms and wool, this striking local concentration must have been the cumulative result of the excellent raw materials available – dyes, mordants, water and wool – together with skilled labour, transport facilities and an efficient marketing system.

Partly because of this concentration, and partly because of the paucity of documentation for the fifteenth–eighteenth centuries, it is very difficult to identify the early products of these centres or to judge how far they were differentiated in appearance. It is scarcely surprising, therefore, that it is generally held to be prudent to ignore the question of where the Anatolian carpets were actually woven, and to adhere to the traditional classifications by pattern, after the Italian and Northern European painters in whose works such carpets often appear. This approach is also reasonable in so far as European taste favoured standard designs, at least for field patterns, the customer's taste being accommodated by appropriate variations in borders. But, unlike Egypt where, at least after the Ottoman conquest of 1516–17, Italian merchants had access to Cairo and, as the Padua synagogue curtain (cf. p. 14) with Hebrew inscription graphically demonstrates,[5] could order special designs, it is more than likely that Italian merchants did not travel to Anatolia at all but were restricted to Istanbul or to ports like Ayasoluk (Altoluogo) near Ephesus, Izmir, Antalya, Lajazzo/Ayas in Cilicia (superseded by Payas in the later sixteenth century) or even to islands like Rhodes or Chios, which remained in Genoese hands practically till the end of Süleymān the Magnificent's reign. Such restrictions can have given very little opportunity to influence or alter the designs, and the influence of external demand must have been principally to determine the weaving of carpets in larger or smaller sizes. If the merchants were

excluded from direct access to the manufacturing centres, there would of course have been agents on the spot or middlemen, but how they worked at the local level is also obscure. It may well be reasonable to assume that large, well-designed and well-executed carpets were the product of permanent workshops located in the larger urban centres, whereas orders for less refined carpets could have been put out to village or even to nomad looms; but in the case of the 'Holbeins' and the 'Lotto' carpets we do not even know how the Ottoman Court looked upon them. The Ottomans tended to disparage the taste of 'foreigners', hence it is quite possible that high Italian fashion was not regarded by them as a luxury at all. But although it is a fair guess that Bergama, Uşak and other Anatolian centres were important sources for such export carpets, the first documented Ottoman association with Uşak relates to the monster carpets ordered for the mosque of Süleymaniye in a letter of 1551; and Bergama, Gördes, Kula, etc. are first documented only in the later seventeenth century.

An additional complication of the carpet market in Ottoman Anatolia is the absence of anything resembling patents at this time, so that popular local designs would have been imitated at any weaving centre capable of copying them, and there might be too few technical or visual peculiarities to distinguish the copies. This is not a problem confined to Anatolia: it applies to European imitations too and, to an even greater extent, to Transylvania and the lower reaches of the Danube, where the Baltic trade in honey, wax, furs, amber and morse ivory debouched, and where a flourishing return trade was conducted in grain, spices, wine and orientalia, including carpets, many of which found their way into the churches and castles of Transylvania and Hungary.

Of the many rug types associated with Transylvania (Siebenbürgen), known both from pieces with a Transylvanian provenance and from Hungarian and other inventories (which are sometimes exceptionally informative on patterns and designs),[6] three are particularly important (more recently augmented, it must be said, with a number of bold and ingenious forgeries): prayer rugs, some with coupled column mihrabs deriving more or less remotely from Cairene Court carpets and with similarities to the eighteenth-century products of Bergama, though often with a two-way symmetrical design with a niche at each end; 'bird' rugs; and rugs with triple spots and tiger-stripes. The 'bird' design is a form of distorted palmette, with parallel forms in some of the tile designs of the mosque of Rüstem Paşa (died 1561) in Istanbul, but the distortion was so convincing that seventeenth-century Ottoman documents refer to them as *karga nakışlı* (with 'crow decoration'), the equivalent description in the Hungarian inventories being *csókás* ('jackdaw').[7] The spots and stripes were a favourite Iranian motif associated with the leopard-skin helmet and tiger-skin coat worn by the hero Rustam and were particularly popular at the Ottoman Court in the later sixteenth century (Ottoman, *peleng nakışlı*; *peleng*, conveniently, meaning both 'leopard' and 'tiger'). Anatolian rugs (and kilims and felts as well) were reaching Transylvania in quantity even by the beginning of the reign of Meḥmed the Conqueror (1451–81), though possibly not via Istanbul, since the trade seems to have been very little affected by the fall of Constantinople in 1453. They were in great demand as wall-hangings, as table carpets, as furnishings for churches and as wedding presents, and in the cities of the Hungarian plain could form part of episcopal tithes, taxes to the Habsburgs and even, paradoxically, tribute to the Ottomans. They had a ceremonial and economic importance, therefore, probably far greater than in contemporary Italy or even in Ottoman Turkey itself, and the local nobility and many churches and monasteries built up large collections of them. Almost certainly, however, quite a lot of these rugs were woven not in Anatolia but locally in Transylvania. For example, marked typological groups among the 'Lotto' rugs have suggested to Charles Grant-Ellis that some were woven, using 'Lotto' designs, in cottage industries in Transylvania or the lower Danube region and transported thence to Central and Northern Europe.[8] Giovanni Curatola has also observed, in a recent study of carpets in Venice (in the Ca' d'Oro, I Frari and the Scuola di San Rocco),[9] that the Turkish carpets, mostly Uşaks of various types, seen in Venice and generally in Italy are typologically distinct from parallel designs found in Hungary and Transylvania. And indeed, if highly creditable versions of medallion- or star-Uşaks could be woven in the late sixteenth and the early seventeenth centuries in England (possibly at Norwich), Spain and Poland (at Białystok),[10] why not in Transylvania too?

A less noticed documentary source is a large medallion-Uşak carpet shown in one of a series of historical tapestries woven for the Wittelsbachs in Munich to designs by Peter Candid, some of them in more than one copy: the first four of the series were ready in February 1609, though the preliminary sketches for the cartoons date from at least five years earlier. An enthronement scene in the complete series of these tapestries in the Wittelsbach palace, the Residenz at Landshut in Upper Bavaria, depicts this carpet, which must have been of splendid proportions and may have been a special commission from Uşak. The series of tapestries also includes a scene depicting Otto von

Wittelsbach receiving an embassy from the Byzantine emperor at the harbour of Ancona in 1158, of which a more brilliant and beautiful version also exists (on loan to the Germanisches Nationalmuseum in Nuremberg).[11] This scene represents a deliberate and systematic exercise in *turquerie*, for the ambassador and his attendants are shown as Ottoman officials, and over his tunic the ambassador wears a kaftan with a rich Bursa medallion-silk design. This attire is depicted with unique accuracy in European painting and, since Peter Candid is not known for his taste for orientalia, it and the other accoutrements must have been treasured pieces from the Wittelsbach collections, most probably acquired on the spot.

If we briefly turn to the sixteenth- and seventeenth-century Ottoman documents, which have already been discussed by Halil Inalcık, our attention is drawn to the inventories of estates of deceased persons (*tereke defterleri*) in the archives of the military kadi's court at Edirne[12] and to a fixed-price list (*narḥ defteri*) for the Istanbul markets drawn up in 1640.[13] These documents are not exactly complementary to the Hungarian, Transylvanian and Italian aristocratic inventories, since they mostly relate to floor-coverings in more general demand; but since it is highly probable that the carpets ordered for or used by the Ottoman Court were not readily available to foreigners, the disparity is perhaps not as great as might at first appear. Similar inventories of personal estates would have been drawn up in kadis' courts all over the Ottoman Empire, but the Edirne series, covering the period 1545–1659, is particularly rich and well preserved.

The inventories give a slightly distorted picture of household effects: for example, a druggist's estate of 1548 – with a house valued at 12,000 akçe and a vast stock of spices, drugs, electuaries, preserves and infusions, and some quite valuable pots – lists no floor-coverings at all. This could have been because estates were disposed of, partially or completely, often by gift during the owner's lifetime. Spouses, moreover, may often have retained ownership of part of the household effects, possibly through a dowry. Those who died while absent from home on a journey or on a campaign must have had estates elsewhere which pass without notice. Alternatively, assets could be seized, for example by creditors, before the kadi's representative arrived to draw up the official inventory, while there must also have been a constant if incalculable drain resulting from peculation or misappropriation. As for the valuations given, it is not surprising that there should be discrepancies with the Istanbul fixed-price register of 1640, even after indexing it for inflation by comparison with the earlier period. This, however, is partly because tacit allowance must generally have been made for condition or age (sometimes there are terse comments such as 'old' or 'worn') and partly because the valuations must reflect sometimes not the expert judgment of the kadi's officials but the actual amounts fetched at auction. That would be reflected, for example, in variable proceeds from the disposal of similar effects, as well as in the relative values of carpets, kilims and felts, the proceeds from which could depend not just upon personal or sentimental preference, but also on short-range local variations in demand.

These somewhat forbidding reflections are a necessary prelude to consideration of the *tereke defter*s, since if one takes the valuation of the dwelling house (most of the houses are town houses in Edirne itself) as an index, the figure for carpets and other floor-coverings amounts to little more than an infinitesimal proportion of it, or of the total amount realized by the estate. For example, that of Yūnus Beg, late governor (*mīrlīva*) of Köstendil (Velbužd) in Serbia, in 1572 totalled more than a million akçe, but the floor-coverings − five prayer carpets (*seccāde*) valued at 724 akçe, Salonike felts at 481 akçe and even a large 'hall' carpet (*ḳālıçe-i dīvān*) at 600 akçe − are mere trifles in comparison with the value of his rich library, his armour, his wardrobe, his personal jewellery and his plate. One gets the impression that these well-to-do people spent far more on dress, for example, than on interior decoration.

In what follows Ömer Lutfî Barkan's published selection of Edirne inventories has been further reduced so as to consider only those inventories in which pile carpets are listed in addition to other floor-coverings, for where there are none the point of comparison is lost. We should first note, in any case, that carpets are a relatively infrequent, though possibly most valuable, type of floor-covering: the others were felts, kilims, occasionally a tiger-skin (*ḳaplān pōstu*), and, from the early-seventeenth century onwards, a heavy napped woollen floor-cloth, *velense* or *velençe* (perhaps from some fancied association with Valencia), manufactured at Karaferye (Verroia) in Thrace, as well as reed matting (*ḥaṣīr, burya*). All these materials were used on occasion for prayer rugs, but the reed mats remind one that the only item of floor-covering specified in the Süleymaniye building accounts, and quite a large amount at that, is *burya-i Mıṣır*, reed mats woven in Egypt or the Northern Sudan: the large carpets ordered for the mosque from Cairo and from the Uşak area were evidently an afterthought. Nor do the Edirne registers show a precise gradation in luxuriousness of floor-coverings, from reed mats up to carpets, as it were. For example, the estate, valued at 217,962 akçe, of a lady, Faṭma Hatun, who died in 1636, lists quilts, cushions

and bolsters luxuriously sewn with pearls and covered with cloth of gold, and also includes two large carpets (2,700 akçe), a striped (*ālāca*) kilim (150 akçe), a small felt and an old one (respectively, 60 akçe and 50 akçe); and Egyptian reed mats, evidently a considerable quantity of them, valued at 120 akçe.

Most floor-coverings are categorized by size − large, medium and small − with, exceptionally, a *nīm seccāde* (a prayer rug, evidently half-sized, not half a rug) valued at 600 akçe, which for a *seccāde* was high. Felts, however, are listed as 'side' felts (*yān kēçesi*), that is runners, 'middle' felts (*orta kēçesi*) and 'divan' felts, this last, like the divan carpet of Yūnus Beg mentioned above, evidently intended for the largest reception room in the house. Though this terminology suggests a gradation in size, the grammar indicates that the 'middle' felts must be for the middle of a room, and some, indeed, are further described as large or small. It is highly probable that the carpets, as in contemporary Italian inventories, also included runners and carpets, possibly round, for the centres of rooms, as well as the largest, most valuable, divan carpets. None is characterized as a table carpet, indicating either that such descriptions occurring in Venetian or Northern European inventories relate only to the use to which they were put in Europe or that table carpets were woven in sizes specially ordered for export and rarely appeared on the local market.

The commonest floor-coverings, which appear even in inventories of estates where there are no carpets listed, were felts (*kebe, kēçe, nemed* − the difference in terminology seems to be a matter of trade terms), some from Iran ('Acem) but the vast majority from Salonike and from Yanbolu in Bulgaria. As usual, little or nothing is said of their decoration, though they are listed by colour or ground-colour − black, white, red, yellow, pale blue (*māī*), *nefṭī* (brown?) and, occasionally, striped (*ālāca*). A few were of fine wool or mohair (*tiftīk*), though these were not among the most valuable, but in general even the richest inhabitants of Edirne owned them. Somewhat surprisingly to modern tastes perhaps, the estate of a Janissary officer (*çāvūṣbāṣı*) in 1568, totalling 253,712 akçe, including several large carpets and two prayer rugs, also features a large selection of 'Acem, Salonike and Yanbolu felts, the valuations of which compare very well with those of the carpets, even with large carpets for which the valuations tend to be disproportionately high. (The 'Acem felts, which are of unknown provenance, tend to be valued at slightly more than the others, but possibly only because, being imports, they involved greater transport and toll costs.) Though felts, as Belon remarked, were made all over the Ottoman Empire and are particularly associated now with Anatolia, Iran and Afghanistan, these Edirne estates corroborate the entries in Ottoman palace inventories of the early sixteenth century in identifying the main supply areas for felts as Thrace and the Balkans. The importance of Salonike in this respect is evidently to be associated with the flourishing woollen industry which largely furnished the Ottoman armies,[14] and Halil Inalcık has recently suggested that both the woollens and the felts are to be associated with Yürük emigration or settlement in the mountains of Northern Greece.

Yürük expansion is also relevant to the kilims, which are, however, less important in terms of both quantity and valuations and tend to come somewhat below the felts. They are rarely described and even their size is rarely indicated, but terms like *kırmızı*, *beyāz* and *ālāca* (red, white, striped) may refer to their grounds. The absence of further specification makes it in fact probable that they originated not from Anatolian centres but from local centres where their style of decoration could be taken for granted. They may well therefore have been woven by the same Yürüks who furnished the Salonike woollens industry.

As for the carpets, which by the early seventeenth century could range in value from 5,000 akçe for a large one to an obviously dreadfully worn piece which fetched only 3 akçe, the largest are generally the most highly valued: these were evidently Anatolian, for a large striped or variegated Egyptian carpet listed in an inventory of mid-August 1606 is valued at only 960 akçe. This last figure may in addition indicate that by this time Egyptian carpets were going out of fashion at the Court and that the makers had turned to supplying the mass market. There are no carpets from Iran, but the absence of designations apart from 'red' or 'white' (the latter, like 'red', referring, perhaps, to a white ground rather than to a plain textile) is striking. The only reference to Uşak, indeed, occurs in an inventory of April 1623 of a dyer (*sabbāğ*), who in fact appears to have been a jeweller too, with a mention of two Uşak prayer rugs valued at 250 and 290 akçe respectively. Other *seccāde*s (to judge from their valuations, pile carpets rather than reed matting, *velense* or felt, which are also mentioned) are designated as 'Egyptian' (*Mısrī*)' On the whole, few prayer carpets are given high valuations, nor does their distribution appear to have been restricted to Muslim households, for the inventory, dated late 1651, of the estate of the (Christian) widow of a rakı distiller, Ḳōstanṭīn b. Vasīlḳō (she survived her husband by only five days), included a *kālīçe seccāde* valued at 107 akçe.

In general, we may conclude from these Edirne inventories that Egyptian carpets were by the early- or mid-seventeenth century less prized than other large

carpets but that even they were owned by relatively few households. This situation appears to have little to do with the size or value of the house itself or of its other furnishings, for carpets are infrequent even in estates with a value totalling more than a million akçe. Possibly the most significant indication of the relatively low status of carpets is to be found in the estate of a rich jeweller at Edirne, Sünbül Ḥasan b. Ḥüseyin: the inventory, drawn up in late-1604, has a total value of almost 940,000 akçe. The deceased owned two large carpets, valued at 1,900 akçe each, two small carpets (335 akçe and 411 akçe) and a worn prayer rug (34 akçe only). Like many jewellers, he was also a pawnbroker and almost half his estate consisted of pledges; these are listed in detail and include gold, silver, items of jewellery, silks and even articles of clothing, but not a single carpet or rug.

The Edirne inventories give nevertheless something of a general picture of the types of floor-coverings used in the houses of the middle classes – merchants, shopkeepers, prosperous craftsmen and Court functionaries – and their relative popularity. Some important complementary information regarding provenances, types and qualities is given in the fixed-price register for the Istanbul markets drawn up in 1640.[15] The character of this register – with its concentration upon locally manufactured goods and with a number of obvious omissions – suggests that it was put together from a series of inspections of the markets by the *mühtesib* (the official with jurisdiction over weights and measures, fair prices, and public order and decency) and his staff, possibly also using information gained by consultation with merchants, and that in some cases trade terms and provenances may be, as usual, difficult to distinguish. It will come as no surprise, however, to those acquainted with Ottoman documents and their deficiencies that Evliyā Çelebī, whose journals are practically contemporary with this register, lists among the carpets stocked by the forty shops of carpet-sellers (*kālīçeciān*) pieces from Izmir, Salonike, Isfahan and Kavala, none of which are mentioned in the fixed-price list. The price levels were fixed to allow a theoretical profit of 10% (sometimes with stated exceptions where the workmanship was particularly minute or where crafts were recognized to be highly labour-intensive). In the case of the rugs and carpets, which were not manufactured in Istanbul but were brought in from the country, that would probably have entailed consultation with the kadis of the various centres to determine the locally fixed prices there, or trust in the merchants' statements or their account books. If there were also middlemen, they would also have received a commission in the region of 10%, but the Istanbul mark-up would also have had to cover transport and packaging costs, as well as the merchants' or their agents' buying trips. One must thus conclude that the prices in the Istanbul register were considerably higher than what the artisans received. None of this price structure appears to have been examined, but there might be something to be learned from cotton manufacture in sixteenth-century Aleppo, where Venetian and other European merchants put out orders for weaving to be carried out in the surrounding villages.[16]

The following extracts relating to floor-coverings of various types are taken from the *narḥ* register:

Prayer rugs:
Seccade Germiyan Kulası Mısır nakışlı / Kula prayer rugs with Cairene decoration: three qualities 1,150, 1,050 and 900 akçe
Germiyan Kulası direk seccade / Kula prayer rug with (double) columns: one quality 650 akçe[17]
Mâlik Paşa tarzı / 'Mâlik Paşa style', larger and smaller sizes, but evidently of a single quality, 950 and 720 akçe
Mıssır'in yedi mihrablı / Cairene prayer rug with 7 mihrabs – evidently placed, to judge from the dimensions, side by side, so a ṣaff, 340 akçe
Selendi'nin peleng nakışlı / Prayer rugs with leopard-spots and tiger-stripes, of two qualities, the higher also being somewhat larger, 280 and 250 akçe
'Acem'in keçe seccadesi / Prayer rugs of Persian felt, 160 akçe
Menteşe'nin mânend-i 'Acem / Felt prayer rugs from Menteşe of Persian appearance or with Persian decoration, 120 akçe
Istanbul'da Üstad Ahmed işe beyaz üzerine nakışlı mânend-i 'Acem keçe seccade / Felt prayer rugs with decoration in Persian style on a white ground made at Istanbul in the factory of Master Aḥmed, 55 akçe.

It is to be noted that locally made felts sell at lower prices, not necessarily because they are inferior in quality but, possibly, because of the greater prestige of imports. Identification by maker, which is a characteristic feature of entries in this *narḥ* register, may suggest that by the mid-seventeenth century there were in Istanbul factories with trade marks, or with products so individual that the use of the name sufficed to identify their wares.

Deve tüyü / Camel-hair prayer rugs, 55 akçe
Selânik hurda nakışlı keçe / Salonike felts with fine decoration, 320 akçe
Selânik iri nakışlı keçe / Salonike felts with bold decoration (Halil Inalcık has suggested *ebrinakışlı* / with cloud decoration), 225 akçe.

Though part of the reason for the higher price of the small-pattern felt was its greater length (3 *dhirā'* rather than 2), the price of the standard-length felt with bold pattern is well up to the prices for Anatolian pile prayer rugs. For these floor-coverings dimensions are more or less standard, so that price differences mostly reflect fashion or popularity or quality, not size. The *dhirā'* – equivalent to the ell – varied from place to place; in Istanbul it was approximately 78 cm.

Carpets:
Uşak red-(ground), in four sizes, from 8,400 akçe, 5,500 akçe, 3,600 akçe to 2,500 akçe
Red-ground Uşaks with a large central medallion (*sofralı*), again in four sizes, from 2,150 akçe, 1,760 akçe, 1,200 akçe and 1,100 akçe; the smallest size is also made in a better quality, to be sold at 1,200 akçe
Medium-sized red-(ground) Uşaks with a central medallion (*sofralı*), larger size 760 akçe, small size 470 akçe
Selendi'nin beyaz üzerine karga nakışlı hammam kaliçesi / Selendi white-ground bird carpets for baths, small size 440 akçe.

Hammam (bath) coverings are also mentioned in the Edirne *tereke defter*s: they cannot have been for the floors of the bath itself, but would have been spread out in the changing room.

Gördüs'ün sarı çatma hammam kaliçesi / Gördes yellow *hammam* carpet, brocaded or embroidered (or possibly, just loosely woven?), small size 400 akçe.

Felts:
Keçe-i 'Acem / Persian felts: large, top quality, 3,920 akçe, medium-sized 880 akçe, and small 840 akçe. (There are no indications of quality for the medium and small sizes.)
Istanbul'da Üstad Ahmed işi mânend-i 'Acem yan keçesi / Side felts or runners with decoration in Persian style made in Istanbul in Master Aḥmed's factory, 110 akçe
Keçe-i Selânik ve Edirne / Salonike and Edirne felts: Salonike, for the middle of a room, in three qualities, 54, 50 and 40 akçe; side felts, longer 84 akçe; shorter 65 (top quality), 60 akçe (medium quality); Edirne, for the middle of a room, top quality 45 akçe; side felts, 53 akçe
Rodos'un orta / Rhodes felts for the middle of a room, top quality 23 akçe; side felts, top quality 44 akçe, medium quality, 40 akçe.

Although Rhodes is normally regarded as having been an entrepôt in the carpet trade, there is also firm evidence that in the seventeenth century it was producing carpets as well: these may have been felts, like those listed here.

Velense (some used not as floor-coverings but as quilts):
Blue and red embroidered Karaferye (Verroia) side velense, 800 akçe
Blue *baṭṭāl* (coarse, low quality, or perhaps just boldly decorated), 680 akçe
Heftrenk baṭṭāl / Multicoloured, large size, 600 akçe, medium-sized, 400 akçe
Orta boy beyaz Karaferye / Medium-sized white Karaferye velense stuffs, 300 akçe
Beyaz baṭṭāl Edirne / Edirne white velense stuffs, 200 akçe
Edirne'nin mai yorgan velensesi / Pale-blue Edirne velense stuff for quilts, 300 akçe; bakkam boyalı / dyed with logwood (*Haematoxylon campechianum*), 280 akçe; red, 250 akçe; white, 180 akçe, but with a heavier quality at 200 akçe
Edirne işi yorgan velensesi / Edirne quilt velense stuffs, 140 akçe; medium-sized, 180 akçe.

Kebe-furūşān / Wares of felt merchants:
Yanbolu'nun mai tiftik kebesi / Pale-blue Yanbolu fine woollen (mohair?) felt, 550 akçe; kırmızı / red, 600 akçe; white, 400 akçe
Yanbolu heftrenk, medium-sized, 200 akçe
Yanbolu heftrenk yan kebesi / Multicoloured Yanbolu side felts, 200 akçe
Tırnova'nın çārkūşe / (?)4-cornered or rectangular (as opposed to round, perhaps) Tirnovo felts, 200 akçe
Tırnova'nin orta boy çārkūşe heftrenk / Multicoloured Tirnovo rectangular(?) felts, 180 akçe
Red, blue and striped (*ālāca*) felts from Lofça in Bulgaria, 80 akçe
Felts from Drama in Thrace: top quality, 40 akçe; medium quality, 30 akçe
Iskelid black felts: plain, 220 akçe; sewn or embroidered, 240 akçe
Eğriboz baṭṭāl boy saçaklı / Fringed Euboea felts: large size, 170 akçe; medium-sized, in three qualities, 90, 80 and 70 akçe; small, 50 akçe
Imroz (Imbros) decorated felts, 45 akçe; lighter weight, top quality, 135 akçe the bundle
Limni (Limnos), top quality felts, sewn with a wide border(?) and in fine strips, 120 akçe the bundle; medium quality, 115 akçe the bundle
Iskelid, top quality, sewn and similarly cut, 115 akçe the bundle, medium quality, 105 akçe the bundle

The *kebe*, as opposed to the *keçe*, pieces also have their weights specified: evidently, the lighter in weight the cheaper. In the later mentions the pricing by bundle may suggest that they were sold unworked and were to be made up into mats, floor-coverings, etc. elsewhere or subsequently.

Kilims:
Germiyan Kulası işi mai deve kilim / Pale-blue (ground) Kula camel kilims, 1,030 akçe
Selendi'nin kırmızı döşeme kilimi / Selendi red floor kilims, 1,000 akçe
Selendi'nin kırmızı deve kilimi / Selendi red camel kilims, 500 akçe
Selendi red kilims, 660 akçe; smaller size 400 akçe
Yassıyurd işi (Yassıyurd work, from an unidentified place, possibly a *yayla* or relating to some nomad territory, but possibly a term used as an Istanbul trade name), red, 240 akçe; smaller size 200 akçe
Demirci işi ālāca / Striped or multi-coloured Demirci kilims, 240 akçe
Yassıyurd işi kırmızı katır kilimi / Yassıyurd red mule kilims, 180 akçe
Demirci işi kırmızı ve yeşil pervazlu sarı saçaklı katır kilimi / Demirci red and green bordered, yellow-fringed mule kilims, 300 akçe; striped 260 akçe; striped camel kilims, 220 akçe
Kula pale-blue (ground) kilims, 630 akçe.

The fixed prices for kilims relate very much to their dimensions, giving values which appear to make no distinction in terms of provenance. There is no evidence in the Edirne *tereke defter*s of kilim or flat-woven horse-, camel- or mule-cloths, though the weaving of such cloths in Anatolia is of considerable antiquity. In fact, some of the camel-cloths listed here are so vast, that those priced at 1,030 and 1,000 akçe may well deserve inverted commas, being called 'camel' kilims on account of their size (7 *dhirā'* by 4 or 6) and meant, notwithstanding, for a large room in a house.

There is also a short entry in the *narḥ* register for *hasır* / reed matting, specified either as *cami'-i şerif* (an honorific term for 'mosque') or in numbers (which are not the dimensions), evidently something akin to the modern Mark I, Mark II, Mark III etc. The most expensive, which are also the largest, are priced at 34 akçe (each); the least, which are also the smallest, at 20 akçe.

For all the importance of felts both in Ottoman society and in the history of Near Eastern and even European floor-coverings, very little is known of their appearance or local peculiarities in times past, and our only recourse is to look at collections of recent felts in ethnographic museums.[18] Extrapolation from such material carries with it the obvious danger that recent or unrecorded changes in nomad or tribal taste may well have completely ousted older patterns; nor were the Turkish nomads and tribal society isolated from interference by the central authorities, including Court demand, even in the sixteenth and seventeenth centuries. Patterns could well, therefore, have changed commensurately with other fabric designs in the same period. Even if patterns have changed considerably, however, it is fairly certain that the decorative techniques employed were persistent and changed, if at all, much less rapidly. The principal techniques which have been noted in Turkey and Western Asia are: (1) decoration fulled into the felt during the process of felting, giving a mosaic effect; (2) decoration painted on when the felting has been completed; (3) decoration by superimposing layers of different colours and cutting away; (4) appliqué decoration with felt or other materials; (5) mosaic decoration with sewn patchwork;[19] (6) decoration by cording or silk bindings; (7) quilting in stitched zigzags or spirals;

and (8) embroidery. All these techniques are known to have existed in ancient times and most can be seen in the famous felts from Pazyryk (Hermitage, Leningrad). It is, however, possible that some of these recorded techniques are geographically restricted, but there is no clear indication of that.[20]

From a study of the Diplomatic Consular Reports of the 1890s M. E. Burkett has concluded[21] that in Iran in the late-nineteenth century felts were principally manufactured at Isfahan, Teheran, Kirman and at some villages in Kirman province. The reports also indicate that Yazd was in earlier years a centre for beautiful felts, some of them large enough to cover a large hall, but that production there had declined considerably. How long Yazd had been famous for its felts is unknown, but it may have been here that the expensive '*Acem* felts in the Ottoman Palace inventories and the Istanbul fixed-price lists were made.

NOTES TO CHAPTER 3

1 Much exploited, most recently by John Mills, 'Near Eastern carpets in Italian paintings' in Robert Pinner and W. B. Denny (eds.), *Carpets of the Mediterranean countries 1400–1600* (London 1986), 109–21; cf. *The Eastern carpet in the Western world from the 15th to the 17th century*, exhibition catalogue (London 1983), *passim*.

2 Michael Rogers, 'Carpets in the Mediterranean countries 1450–1550. Some historical observations' in *Carpets of the Mediterranean countries* (op. cit.), 13–28. For the later engravings cf. *La processione del Doge nella Domenica delle Palme, incisa in Venezia per Mattio Pagan (1556–1569)*, (Venice 1880).

3 P. Belon du Mans, *Les observations de plusieurs singularitez* (Paris 1588), fol. 182b.

4 Halil Inalcık, 'The Yürüks: Their origins, expansion and economic role' in *Carpets of the Mediterranean countries*, op. cit., 39–65; Julian Raby, 'Court and export: Part I. Market demands in Ottoman carpets 1450–1550', ibid., 29–38.

5 A. Boralevi, 'Un tappeto ebraico Italo-Egiziano', *Critica d'Arte* XLIX (1984), 34–47.

6 V. Gervers, *The influence of Ottoman Turkish textiles and costume in Eastern Europe* (Royal Ontario Museum, Toronto 1982), 23–32, 43–7; M. B. Nagy, *Reneszánsz és barokk Erdélyben* (Renaissance and Baroque in Transylvania), (Bucharest 1970).

7 E. Schmutzler, *Altorientalische Teppiche in Siebenbürgen* (Leipzig 1932); Albert Eichhorn, 'Kronstadt und der orientalische Teppich', *Forschungen zur Volks- und Landeskunde* X (Bucharest 1967), 72–84; Ferenc Batári, 'White ground Anatolian carpets in the Budapest Museum of Applied Arts' in *Carpets of the Mediterranean countries*, op. cit. (note 1), 195–203. The *karga–csókás* consonance is remarkable, but curious, for in Anatolia *karga* is an ill-omened bird. We might thus conclude that *karga nakışlı* is an Ottoman calque upon the Hungarian, perhaps indicating an export design, or at least implying that unbelievers deserved any ill-omened carpets they got.

8 C. G. Ellis, 'The ''Lotto'' patterns as a fashion in carpets' in *Festschrift für Peter Wilhelm Meister* (Hamburg 1975), 19–31; id., 'On ''Holbein'' and ''Lotto'' rugs' in *Carpets of the Mediterranean countries*, op. cit. (note 1), 163–76.

9 Giovanni Curatola, 'Four carpets in Venice', ibid., 123–30.

10 A factory appears to have been set up there on the initiative of Krzysztof Wiesiołowski, who became Grand Master of Lithuania in 1535 and died in 1537. Cf. *The Eastern carpet in the Western world*, op. cit. (note 1), No. 42.

11 Brigitte Volk-Knüttel, *Wandteppiche für den Münchener Hof nach Entwürfen von Peter Candid*, exhibition catalogue (Deutscher Kunstverlag, Berlin, 1976), Nos. 3–4.

12 Ö. L. Barkan, 'Edirne askerî kassam'ına ait tereke defterleri (1545–1659)', *Belgeler* III (Ankara 1966), 1–479.

13 M. S. Kütükoğlu, *Osmanlılarda narh müessesesi ve 1640 narh defteri* (Istanbul 1983), especially 178–85.

14 Halil Sahillioğlu, 'Yeniçeri çuhası ve II. Bayazid'in son yıllarında Yeniçeri çuha muhasebesi', *Güney-Doğu Avrupa Araştırmaları Dergisi* 2–3 (Istanbul 1973–4), 415–67; Suraiya Faroqhi, 'Textile production in Rumeli and the Arab provinces: Geographical distribution and internal trade (1560–1650)', *Osmanlı Araştırmaları/The Journal of Ottoman Studies* I (Istanbul 1980), 61–83.

15 Op. cit. (note 13).

16 Ugo Tucci (ed.), *Lettres d'un marchand vénitien, Andrea Berengo (1553–1556)*, (Paris 1957).

17 Cf. M. S. Beattie, 'Coupled-column prayer rugs', *Oriental Art* XIV (1968), 243–58.

18 M. E. Burkett, *The art of the felt weaver*, exhibition catalogue (Kendal 1979).

19 Though executed in leather, not in felt, an important document for this particular technique exists in the shape of a leather canteen with red, white and blue arabesques, interlaces and cloud-collars which must reproduce a sophisticated felt design. It was presented c.1580 by Murād III to the Habsburg emperor, Rudolf II, who put it into his renowned Kunstkammer; it is now in the Kunsthistorisches Museum, Vienna (C.28). Cf. *The Age of Süleyman the Magnificent*, exhibition catalogue (Washington, D.C. 1987), No. 105.

20 Berthold Laufer, 'The early history of felt', *American Anthropologist* NS 32 (1930), 1–18; Michael and Veronika Gervers, 'Felt-making craftsmen of the Anatolian and Iranian plateaux', *Textile Museum Journal* IV/1 (Washington, D.C. 1974), 14–29; Yusuf Durul, 'Keçe sanatı', *IVᵉ Congrès International d'Art Turc* (Aix-en-Provence 1976), 67–8.

21 *The art of the felt weaver*, op. cit.

Illustrations 1–45:

TURKISH AND CAIRENE CARPETS

CAPTIONS AND NOTES TO ILLUSTRATIONS
1–45

1 Prayer rug, formerly associated with Sultan Aḥmed I (1603–17), warps undyed wool, wefts yellow wool, Persian knot, 49 knots per square cm, pile wool, probably Cairo, later-sixteenth or early-seventeenth century; 13/2037. Dimensions 190 × 140 cm.

The field is a mihrab niche with a central pointed medallion composed of a stylized chinoiserie lotus, gracefully drooping feathery leaves and Prunus blossoms, with a lobed arch and corner-pieces at the base filled with dense spiral arabesque scrolling. The spandrels, which have been almost eliminated from the composition, have cloud-scroll filling. The border is a broken scroll with composite chinoiserie peony- and lotus-heads, swirling feathery leaves and half-blossoms giving a strong, if jerky, undulating movement. The guard stripes are of rosettes between thin bands of meander. The overall design is vertically symmetrical and associates this rug with the well-known group of Court carpets, often, though so far inconclusively, attributed to a workshop in either Istanbul or Bursa.

The rug has suffered considerable damage from being stored while carelessly folded.

☐ *The Anatolian Civilisations*, exhibition catalogue (Istanbul 1983), E 239, with references. Here it is stated that the rug was taken from the tomb of Selīm II (died 1574) at Ayasofya in Istanbul, though the earliest source for this – E. Kuhnel, *Die Sammlung Türkischer und Islamischer Kunst im Tschinili Köschk* (Berlin-Leipzig 1938), Plate 37 – states merely that the rug was removed in 1885 'from the tomb of Selīm', without saying whether it was that of Selīm I (died 1520), Selīm II or Selīm III (died 1807). On the basis of date, the tomb of Selīm II is the most plausible, but the rug could have been placed there later. This does not therefore preclude an association with Aḥmed I, or with anyone else, though for the moment that must be left in suspense. For a discussion of the value of such provenances, see J. M. Rogers (ed.), *The Topkapı Saray Museum, Costumes, Embroideries and other Textiles* (London and Boston, Mass. 1986), 12.

2 Prayer rug, warps undyed wool, wefts deep-blue wool, Persian knot, 100 knots per square cm, pile wool, Istanbul, or possibly Hereke, nineteenth century, with seventeenth-century motifs; 13/2023. Dimensions 145 × 98 cm.

The field is an elaborately lobed mihrab niche with a highly decorated lamp and a lobed medallion in the centre on a ground of imbricated cloud-bands and spiral trails of chinoiserie lotus. The spandrels and corner-pieces at the base have a more elaborate lotus-scroll, with two medallions filled with inscriptions; these have not been satisfactorily read, though it has been claimed that they bear the signature of a craftsman, Maḥmūd al-Kirmānī. At the head of the mihrab niche is a panel of fine rounded script reading *Allahumma*

ṣalla ‘alā Muḥammad ṣāḥib al-tāj wa’l-mi‘rāj wa’l-mabarr [? for *mabarra*] *wa’l-miḥrāb wa ‘alā āl Muḥammad wa* [one word unread] *wa salama*, impromptu prayers (*du‘ā*) invoking blessings upon Muḥammad and his descendants. Such is most probably the content also of the medallion in each spandrel. The border is of lotus-medallions and split palmettes having close similarities to sixteenth-century border illuminations. The guard bands are a double undulating scroll.

Though many of the individual motifs are drawn from sixteenth-century manuscript illumination, the design is indebted, as is the colour-scheme, to the great sixteenth-century Uşak carpets ordered for the Imperial mosques of Istanbul. These of course continued to be copied, with little alteration, in the seventeenth century and even in the eighteenth century. The composition is also related to Bergama and Uşak prayer rugs of the seventeenth–eighteenth centuries.

This fine piece has suffered damage from being stored while folded down the vertical axis.

3 Prayer rug, warps undyed wool, wefts deep-blue wool, Persian knot, 64 knots per square cm, pile wool, Istanbul, or possibly Hereke, nineteenth century, in archaizing style; 13/2032. Dimensions 135 × 95 cm.

The field is a mihrab niche with a lobed pointed arch and with conspicuous corner-pieces at the base, with a stylized hanging ornament and bold medallion in the centre. Spandrels, corner-pieces and medallion are filled with scrolling of split palmettes, bichrome and almost modelled. The ground is a chinoiserie lotus-trail deriving from large medallion Uşak carpets of the sixteenth century. Above the mihrab is a panel of *du‘ā* in rounded script: *Qāl Allāhu ta‘ālā ‘ajjalū bi’l-ṣalwat* [sic] *qabl al-fawt, wa ‘ajjalū al-tawba* [sic] *qabl al-mawt*, a somewhat incorrectly transcribed prayer (which occurs on several carpets in this group) translated as 'God has said, may He be exalted, "Hasten to prayer before passing (away) and hasten to repentance before death"'. The border is a much simplified version of a Court carpet border (as seen, for example, in *No. 1*), featuring lotuses and a spiral scroll with cloud-bands superimposed. The outer guard stripe is a hooked running scroll.

The rug has suffered damage from being stored while folded down the centre.

continued on page 130

1

3

4

5

6

8

9

12

13

15

21

22

28

29

30

34

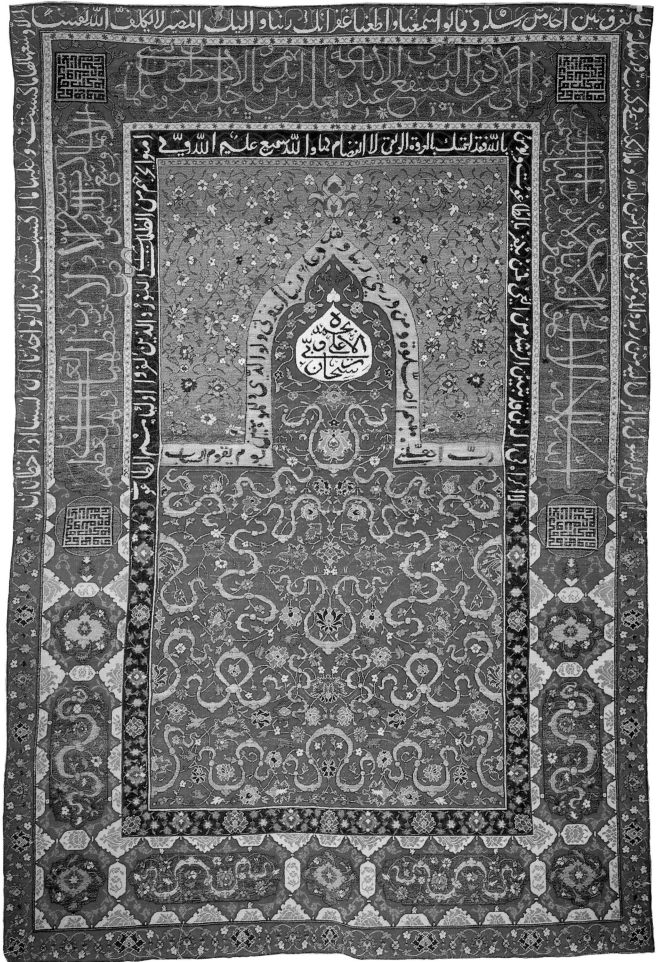

36

37

39

40

42

4 Prayer rug, warps undyed pale café-au-lait wool, wefts deep-blue wool, Persian knot, 36 knots per square cm, pile wool, Istanbul, or possibly Hereke, nineteenth century, in archaizing style; 13/2038. Dimensions 136 × 90 cm.

The field is a mihrab niche with pointed lobed arch and elaborately bulging consoles, the latter in lieu of side columns. The filling is all-over arabesque in a grid pattern, somewhat reminiscent of the design of 'Lotto' carpets. The spandrels also have arabesque filling with rather well-drawn split palmettes. Above the mihrab is a panel with, in simple rounded script without much pointing (*haraka*), a form of Shī'ī *shahāda*: *Lā ilāh ilā'llāh, Muhammad rasūl Allāh: Allāh:* '*Alī walī Allāh ḥaqqan ḥaqqan* / 'There is no god but God, Muhammad is His prophet, 'Alī is the friend of God, in truth, in truth.' At the apex of the mihrab niche is a pointed oval medallion with 'Allāh', 'Muhammad' and a number of meaningless or illegible signs. The border is a zigzag, highly stylized lotus-scroll with equally stylized chinoiserie cloud-bands between. The guard stripes are bands of thin scroll.

While the filling is somewhat comparable to that of the mihrab niche seen in *No. 30*, the stark colour-scheme is perhaps closer to those of *Nos. 32* and *33*.

5 Prayer rug, warps bright-pink wool, wefts light-blue cotton, Persian knot, 49 knots per square cm, pile wool, Istanbul, or possibly Hereke, nineteenth century, in archaizing style; 13/2029. Dimensions 160 × 100 cm.

The field is a mihrab niche with heavily lobed pointed arch and, below, corner-pieces so exaggerated as to make the design almost symmetrical, in the manner of some 'Transylvanian' prayer rugs. The centre of the niche contains a lobed medallion with double pendants filled with arabesques of very stiff cloud-scrolls, and with *Allāhu akbar* / 'God is All-great' at the apex. The filling of the medallion is a knotted cloud-band superimposed upon a rather stiff, almost spiral, floret-scroll, while the ground is of black split palmettes contoured in bright red over a series of similarly stiff spiral scrolls. The spandrels and corner-pieces are of gaudy cloud-bands over floral scrolls copied at some distance from the 'International Timurid' repertoire, and the border is a variation upon the same elements, cloud-bands knotted or separated over thinner scroll motifs.

Above the niche is a panel of rather lax rounded script, somewhat comparable to that seen in *No. 4*, characterized by exaggerated *shāddas* which interrupt the ductus, in a form of Shī'ī *shahāda*: *Lā ilāh ilā'llāh Muhammad rasūl Allāh 'Alī walī*

Allāh ḥaqqan ḥaqqan / 'There is no god but God, Muhammad is God's prophet, 'Alī is the friend of God, in truth, in truth.'

6 Prayer rug, warps undyed wool, wefts pale-blue wool, Persian knot, 36 knots per square cm, pile wool. Istanbul, or possibly Hereke, nineteenth century, in archaizing style; 13/2020. Dimensions 136 × 90 cm.

The field is a lobed mihrab niche, practically symmetrical though with contrasting ground colours above and below, with in the centre a lobed lozenge medallion and pendants with symmetrically disposed frilly cloud-bands and a network of chinoiserie lotus-scroll. The corner-pieces and spandrels have rather angular palmettes. The plain ground is cinnamon-coloured. The border is of fat knotted cloud-scrolls, quite discrete, on a trailing scroll with chinoiserie lotus. Above the mihrab niche is a panel of rounded script: '*Ajjalū bi'l-ṣalwa qabl al-fawt wa 'ajjalū bi'l-tawba qabl al-mawt*, grammatically correct, though with the words somewhat peculiarly broken up.

The border and medallion designs are greatly indebted to smaller medallion Uṣaks of the sixteenth and seventeenth centuries, but the stiffer effect is more reminiscent of eighteenth-century Bergama rugs.

The rug has suffered considerable damage from being stored while folded lengthwise.

7 Prayer rug, warps pale-pink wool, wefts pale-green wool, Persian knot, 100 knots per square cm, pile wool, enhanced with metal thread. The upper border has a flat-weave strip bearing verses by an unidentified poet. Istanbul, or possibly Hereke, nineteenth century, in archaizing style; 13/2030. Dimensions 160 × 112 cm.

The three inscription borders are all Koranic: the outer one is XXVII, 30 + VI, 83–4; the principal inscription border is II, 255, complete; the inner one is XXIV, 35. The mihrab arch bears XVII, 78 + IV, 103 + LXVIII, 51–2. At the apex of the niche is *Allāhu akbar kabīran* / 'God is All great, greatly,' while the spandrels bear selections from the *Asmā' Allāh al-Ḥusnā* / the '99 Names of God'.

The field is a mihrab niche featuring an exaggeratedly pointed horseshoe arch, within which a decorated vase is flanked by stylized cypresses and Prunus blossom, the vase resting on a sort of mat and having a wreath-like bouquet in it. The ground is of thin spiral scrolls, some with stylized chinoiserie lotuses and confronted cloud-bands. The main border is a bold split-palmette scroll with modelled forms and with detached cloud-bands on a ground of very fine spiral blossom-scroll, after sixteenth-century manuscript illumination. The guard stripes are of double scrolls. The medallions of square Kufic are in pairs, those on the left-hand side being reversed. The upper pair bear the latter part of Koran XXI, 87, and the lower pair the latter part of XI, 88 (but missing the final word of the verse).

The vegetation flanking the vase derives from similar cypresses and Prunus branches occurring on Tabriz carpets of the sixteenth century, for example the Chelsea carpet in the Victoria and Albert Museum, London.

8 Prayer rug, warps and wefts yellow wool, Persian knot, 100 knots per square cm, pile wool enhanced with metal thread, Istanbul, or possibly Hereke, nineteenth century, in archaizing style; 13/2040. Dimensions 160 × 120 cm.

The triple inscription border, which is of finely drawn and well-contrasted rounded scripts, is entirely Koranic: the outermost is XXVII, 30 + VI, 83; the main inscription is the Āyat al-Kursī, II, 255, though in bold script only as far as *al-samāwāt wa'l-arḍ* (the rest of the verse being continued, much smaller, outside the panel); the inner band is XXIV, 35. Less fine is the dense inscription on the arch of the mihrab, Koran XVII, 78 + IV, 103 + LXVIII, 51–2. The panelled spandrels bear select '99 Names of God', while at the apex of the niche is *Allāhu akbar kabīran*/'God is All-great, greatly'. The panels of square Kufic are in pairs, none of them reversed. The upper ones include assorted ejaculatory prayers: *subḥānahu Allāh wa'l-ḥamdu li'llāh wa lā ilāh ilā'llāh wa Allāhu akbar*, possibly with some otiose letters. The lower panels announce that they are *ḥadīth*, but the actual *ḥadīth*, around the outside, has not been read.

The field is an elaborate mihrab niche, with a constricted pointed horseshoe arch, having at the centre a decorated vase containing a mandorla-like floral bouquet. Below this is an elaborate composite inverted-lotus medallion flanked by stylized cypresses and flowering Prunus, with small naturalistic flowers below and a fine spiral-scroll ground. Above are confronted heavily imbricated and wriggling cloud-bands. The main border is of medallions with palmette filling alternating with notched stems filled with chinoiserie lotus-stems in 'International Timurid' style; the ground is of thin foliate trails. This border design is very reminiscent of seventeenth-century Safavid tilework on the monuments of Meshed in Khurasan, but it is possible that both designs have a common origin in manuscript illumination. The filling of the mihrab niche, however, is much more in the tradition of sixteenth-century North-West Persian carpet design. The inner guard stripe is merely a thin band of foliate scroll.

In its design and drawing this piece is one of the most splendid of the group, though the eclecticism and abundance of motifs is almost overpowering.

9 Prayer rug, warps and wefts yellow wool, Persian knot, 100 knots per square cm, pile wool enhanced with metal thread, Istanbul, or possibly Hereke, nineteenth century, in archaizing style; 13/2009. Dimensions 170 × 116 cm.

The three border inscriptions are all Koranic: the outer one is XXVII, 30 + VI, 83–4 (as far as the word *Dā'ūd*); the main border is the Āyat al-Kursī, II, 255, complete; and the inner border is XXIV, 35. The mihrab arch is inscribed with XVII, 78 + IV, 103 + LXVIII, 51–2. The panels of square Kufic are in pairs, each with the left-hand panel reversed: the upper pair have the latter part of XXI, 87, and the lower pair XI, 88 (but missing the final word).

The field and border designs are for all practical purposes a replica of those seen in *No. 7*, though with an entirely different colour scheme and slightly different dimensions. The only significant detail of difference, suggesting a degree

of redrawing of the cartoon, or a degree of disobedience on the part of the weaver, is the small 'islands' on which the cypresses and the Prunus branches stand. It is possible that this rug and *No. 7* were woven as a pair.

10 Prayer rug, warps and wefts of yellow wool, with a supplementary white cotton warp every 15 cm, Persian knot, 81 knots per square cm, pile wool, enhanced with metal thread, Istanbul, or possibly Hereke, nineteenth century, in archaizing style; 13/2162. Dimensions 163 × 114 cm.

The three inscription borders are all Koranic, though in scripts approaching *nasta'līq*: the outer border is II, 285–6, complete; the main inscription is II, 255, complete; the inner band is praise of the Fourteen (Shī'ī) Immaculates, that is Muḥammad, Fāṭima and the Twelve Shī'ī Imams. The mihrab arch bears Koran XVII, 78 + IV, 103 + LXVIII, 51–2. There are two panels of square Kufic, neither of them reversed. The upper pair are evidently *ḥadīth*, since at the centre they have *Qāl al-nabī 'alayhi al-salām*/'The Prophet, praise be upon him, said', but the outer clockwise inscription has not been read. The lower pair are miscellaneous *du'ā*: *subḥānahu Allāh wa'l-ḥamdu li'llāh wa lā ilāh ilā'llāh* [with some otiose letters, it would seem] *wa Allāhu akbar*. The spandrels of the mihrab are filled with select '99 Names of God', after the same or similar cartoons to *Nos. 7* and *9*. At the apex of the niche is a distorted *nasta'līq* panel; *Muḥammad 'Alī Allāh*.

The field is a mihrab niche with panelled spandrels and a filling of a decorated hanging vase with a medallion above suggesting a mandorla. The ground is of stiff pomegranate and Prunus branches of trees and discrete cloud-bands symmetrically disposed about the vertical axis and is a coarser version of the ground of *No. 20*. The main border is a more polychrome version of that of *No. 9* and other carpets of this group, in which cloud-bands, split palmettes and thin spiral blossom-scrolls appear in utter confusion. The guard stripes are a jerkily undulating scroll with chinoiserie lotus-heads.

11 Prayer rug, warps and wefts of pale-yellow wool, Persian knot, 100 knots per square cm, pile wool enhanced with silver thread, Istanbul, or possibly Hereke, nineteenth century, in archaizing style; 13/2018. Dimensions 163 × 108 cm.

There are only two, instead of the usual three, inscription borders: the outer one is spidery and illegible; the inner one, also spidery but in a script reminiscent of the main border of *No. 7*, is the Āyat al-Kursī, Koran II, 255. The inscription on the mihrab is Koran LIX, 23–4, the remaining space being filled by select '99 Names of God', which also fill the panels of the spandrels. The medallions with square Kufic above have a compressed version of the lower medallions of *No. 9*, Koran XI, 88 (the latter part of the verse).

The field is a mihrab niche, with exaggerated pointed horseshoe arch, having at the centre a decorated vase on an inverted crown, with confronted fruiting pomegranate trees below and flowering trees above, together with fat chinoiserie clouds at the base of the arch. These are on a ground of fine spiral chinoiserie lotus-scroll. At the apex of the arch is an inscription panel with *Allāhu akbar kabīran*/'God is All-great, greatly'. The main border is of rosettes and oblong cartouches with palmettes or a complex double-spiral scroll in which split palmettes, very finely drawn, seem to be superimposed on a thinner blossom-scroll: the inscription cartouches have only this latter scroll ground. The panels are set on a contrasting ground of chinoiserie floral scroll. The field design is related in various ways to those of *Nos. 10* and *20*.

12   Prayer rug, warps and wefts yellow wool, Persian knot, 100 knots per square cm, pile wool enhanced with silver thread, Istanbul, or possibly Hereke, nineteenth century, in archaizing style; 13/2021. Dimensions 160 × 103 cm.
The three border inscriptions are all Koranic: the outermost, in an extraordinarily arranged spidery script, is II, 285–6; the main border, which is better drawn but very badly arranged, is II, 255; and the inner one, in quasi-*nasta'līq* which is also spidery, is III, 18–20. The quasi-*nasta'līq* inscription (in a fatter hand) on the mihrab arch is XIV, 40–1. The *nasta'līq* inscriptions virtually lack pointing (*ḥaraka*) and have practically no dotting (*tashkīl*) either. The panels of square Kufic below (the left-hand panel reversed) have the latter part of XXI, 87. At the very apex of the mihrab niche is *Allāhu akbar kabīran*/'God is All-great, greatly'.
The field is a mihrab niche with exaggerated pointed horseshoe arch, having at the centre a fat lobed medallion filled with split-palmette scrolls, with a trefoil finial and a base in the form of an inverted crown. The ground is of chinoiserie floral scrolls. The spandrels of the mihrab are filled with scale-like panels, each with one or more of the '99 Names of God', written clockwise from the point of the arch so that most are upside down vis-à-vis the viewer. The border is a thin undulating scroll with wriggling cloud-bands superimposed. The guard stripes are chinoiserie floral scrolls.
In terms of the content of its inscriptions, the medallion filling of the mihrab niche and even some of the scripts, this rug is a less refined version of *No. 13*.

13   Prayer rug, warps and wefts yellow wool, Persian knot, 100 knots per square cm. pile wool, enhanced with metal thread, Istanbul, or possibly Hereke, nineteenth century, in archaizing style; 13/2035. Dimensions 165 × 115 cm.
The three inscription borders, which are entirely Koranic, are a conjunction of a rather ill-drawn central inscription (II, 255), which does not succeed in turning corners, between inscriptions in quasi-*nasta'līq*, the outer one II, 285–6, and inner one XVII, 78–9. On the mihrab arch, also in a sort of *nasta'līq*, is Koran XIV, 40–1. The two panels of square Kufic are the latter part of Koran XXI, 87. At the apex of the niche is *Allāhu akbar kabīran*/'God is All-great, greatly'.
The field is a mihrab niche with constricted pointed horseshoe arch and spandrels filled with scale-like panels thinly overlaid with spiral foliate scrolls and cloud-bands. At the centre of the niche is a bloated decorated vase on a base in the form of an inverted crown, filled with floral motifs in crown-like compartments, on a ground of thick, rather coarse chinoiserie lotus-scroll heavily brocaded with metal thread.

The main border, which is very typical of the whole group in the Topkapı Saray, is of split palmette-scrolls and wriggling cloud-bands superimposed on a finer spiral scroll. The colour contrasts here enhance the drawing of the motifs. The guard stripes are of double undulating palmette- or lotus-scrolls.

14   Prayer rug, warps and wefts yellow wool, Persian knot, 100 knots per square cm, pile wool enhanced with metal thread, Istanbul, or possibly Hereke, nineteenth century, in archaizing style; 13/2019. Dimensions 158 × 114 cm.
The three inscription borders are all Koranic: the outermost, in quasi-*nasta'līq* is II, 285–6; the middle border, in carelessly pointed, rather angular thin script which does not appear to know how to turn corners, is II, 255 (with dittography of the words *al-'ālī* at the end); the inner one, in a quasi-*nasta'līq* somewhat similar to that of *No. 12*, is III, 18–19. The passage on the mihrab arch is also similar to its counterpart on *No. 12*, both in script and content, XIV, 40–1. The spandrels are filled with scale-like panels crammed with select '99 Names of God', in the form of invocations. At the apex of the mihrab niche is an inscription (damaged) of praise of God (. . . *subḥān al-a'lā bi-ḥamdihi*).
The field is a mihrab niche with pointed horseshoe arch and with a central bloated vase composed of crown motifs on a base or mat in the form of an inverted crown, and having above it a small envelope or portfolio which may or may not be represented as hanging from chains. The ground is of undulating lotus-scrolls superimposed upon a very fine spiral blossom-scroll. The main border is of rosettes and transverse panels alternating with oblong cartouches, the latter filled with lax chinoiserie cloud-bands. The alternating cartouches and panels are paralleled on the Yerkes carpet (cf. p. 27), but the effect here is fussy and the treatment of the motifs suggests that the weaver had no clear idea of what he was doing.

15   Prayer rug, warps red wool, wefts white wool, Turkish knot, 42 knots per square cm, pile wool, Istanbul or possibly Hereke, nineteenth century, in archaizing style; 13/2051. Dimensions 180 × 118 cm.
The main inscription, rather ill-drawn and arranged, is the Āyat al-Kursī, Koran II, 255. The outer and inner inscriptions, both in quasi-*nasta'līq* scripts, are Persian *munājāt*, informal or non-canonical meditations upon God. The mihrab arch bears Koran XIV, 40–1, while the spandrels have rather sparse panels with invocations of some of the '99 Names of God'. The panels of square Kufic all have the same text – the latter part of Koran XXXI, 87 – the two on the right being reversed. At the apex of the niche is *Allāhu akbar*/'God is All-great'.
The field is a mihrab niche with pointed horseshoe arch, having at the centre a decorated vase with a crown-like calyx foot and a crown-like collar at the neck, from which springs a vertically symmetrical split palmette-scroll, the palmettes being bichrome and almost modelled in effect. The scroll overlies a thinner spiral lotus-scroll. The main border is an undulating notched stem with foliate heads, rather cramped at the base, filled with 'International Timurid' chinoiserie

lotuses and on a ground of thin foliate trails. The guard stripes are similar chinoiserie motifs but more stylized, in scroll form, the outer band being markedly stiff and angular.

The occurrence of Persian devotional inscriptions on this and other rugs in the Topkapı Saray collections – some of them with reference to the Pilgrimage, and some, though not all, Sufi in content – is a reminder of the origins and the diffusion of the prayer carpet as such. Its use does not go back to the time of the Prophet, but may have been introduced from the eastern lands of Islam, or even from the Buddhist cultures of Eastern Asia, as late as the eleventh century AD. It was particularly associated with the Sufi orders, whose heads were often given the title of *shaykh al-sajjāda* (the shaykh of the prayer carpet), and its establishment in the west of Islam may well have been the work of Sufi orders, many of them Turkish, which came from the east in the wake of the Turkish invasions of the eleventh to fourteenth centuries.

☐ Cf. Hanna Erdmann, "Die Matte muss alt sein". Zur Kulturgeschichte des Gebetsteppichs', *Festschrift für Peter Wilhelm Meister zum 65.Geburtstag* (Hamburg 1975), 11–18.

16 Prayer rug, warps and wefts pale-yellow wool, Persian knot, 100 knots per square cm, pile wool enhanced with metal thread, Istanbul, or possibly Hereke, nineteenth century, in archaizing style; 13/2013. Dimensions 164 × 110 cm.

Of the three inscriptions only the main inscription, in rather cramped *thuluth*, is Koranic (II, 255). The outer and inner inscriptions, both in quasi-*nasta'līq* hands, are Persian *munājāt*. The mihrab arch, also in quasi-*nasta'līq*, is Koran XIV, 40–1. At the apex of the niche is *Allāhu akbar*/'God is All-great', while the spandrels bear select '99 Names of God' in the form of invocations. The four panels of square Kufic all have the latter part of Koran XXI, 87 (reversed on the right).

The field is a mihrab niche with, at the centre, an elaborately decorated vase on a trefoil inverted-crown base; the vase has a fine composite chinoiserie lotus filling, a crown collar at the neck, and an inverted composite wreath-like lotus above. The ground is of 'International Timurid' spiral lotus-scrolls, with cloud-bands superimposed, confronted and generally vertically symmetrical. The border is of notched undulating stems and foliate heads filled with scrollwork, also in 'International Timurid' style, on a ground of thin foliate trails. The motifs are more characteristic of Safavid than of Ottoman illumination in the sixteenth century, but may well derive from Uşak carpet designs. The guard stripes are undulating floral scrolls.

The inscriptions and some of the design elements suggest that this is a finer version of *No. 15*. Since the cartoons would have been drawn so as to produce the finest effect, *No. 15* should be regarded as the copy and this as the prototype.

17 Prayer rug, warps yellow wool, wefts white cotton, Persian knot, 81 knots per square cm, pile wool enhanced with silver thread, Istanbul, or possibly Hereke, nineteenth century, in archaizing style; 13/2161. Dimensions 173 × 117 cm.

The outer two of the three inscription borders are Koranic: outermost II, 285–6; and the main inscription, in bold quasi-*nasta'līq*, II, 255. The inner inscription consists of prayers for blessings upon the Fourteen Shīʿī Immaculates. The mihrab arch is framed by Koran XVII, 78 + IV, 103 + LXVIII, 51–2. The spandrels are filled with panels bearing some of the '99 Names of God'. Like those of the mihrab arch, they are identical, and in identical scripts to the corresponding inscriptions on *No. 10*. The pairs of panels of square Kufic are also very similar, but their positions have been reversed, with unidentified *ḥadīth* below and assorted *duʿā*, chosen doubtless because the letter forms could easily be accommodated to the square Kufic style: *subḥān[ahu] Allāh wa'l-ḥamdu li'llāh wa lā ilāh ilā'llāh wa Allāhu akbar*, possibly with some otiose letters. At the head of the mihrab arch is a panel with *Allāhu akbar kabīran*/'God is All-great, greatly'.

The field is a mihrab niche with constricted pointed horseshoe arch and a filling, related to *Nos. 16* and *18*, of medallions and pendants on a fine spiral scroll ground, overlaid with long writhing imbricated cloud-bands, bichrome split palmettes and chinoiserie lotus-heads, all lavishly worked with metal thread. The design is vertically symmetrical. The border is a somewhat weaker version of that of *No. 2*, while the guard stripes are of double undulating scrollwork with lotuses and cloud-bands.

18 Prayer rug, warps yellow wool, wefts up to 9 cm from the edges pink wool, those in the centre being yellow wool, Persian knot, 100 knots per square cm, pile wool, enhanced with metal thread, Istanbul, or possibly Hereke, nineteenth century, in archaizing style; 13/2042. Dimensions 165 × 105 cm.

The three inscription borders are all Koranic, in contrasting competent, if rather thinly drawn, rounded scripts: the outer one is II, 285–6; the main border is the Āyat al-Kursī, II, 255, complete; and the inner one VII, 204–6. That of the mihrab arch, which is rather fuzzy in effect, appears to be Koran LIX, 23–4, the remaining space being filled by various of the '99 Names of God'. These also fill the scale-like panels of the spandrels, mostly in pairs (hence, some of them are reminiscent of the Koranic verses in which the two names jointly appear) in well-drawn rounded script, but most of them upside down vis-à-vis the viewer. At the apex of the mihrab niche, also upside down, is a cartouche with *Allāhu akbar kabīran*/'God is All-great, greatly'. The main inscription border is punctuated by four panels of square Kufic, which are in pairs, those on the right-hand side being reversed. The upper pair bear the latter part of Koran XXI, 87; the lower pair have Koran XI, 88, the latter part also but seemingly omitting the final word.

The field is a mihrab niche with constricted pointed horseshoe arch filled with well-drawn cloud-bands symmetrical on both axes on a rather dense spiral chinoiserie lotus-scroll. The main border is a double scroll with split palmettes boldly superimposed upon a dense spiral scroll with small florets and stylized chinoiserie lotuses, rather weakly realized.

This particular design was woven in at least one more example, which is now in the Metropolitan Museum, New York, Fletcher Collection, 17.120.124. Cf. M. Dimand and Jean Mailey, *Oriental rugs in the Metropolitan Museum of Art* (New York 1973), No. 48.

19 Prayer rug, warps and wefts yellow wool, Persian knot, 100 knots per square cm, pile wool, enhanced with metal thread. The ends have flat-woven borders 1·5 cm deep with unidentified verses woven into them. Istanbul, or possibly Hereke, nineteenth century, in archaizing style; 13/2163. Dimensions 168 × 111 cm.
Of the three inscription borders the outermost seems to be non-Koranic and in Persian. The main inscription is the Āyat al-Kursī, Koran II, 255, complete; the innermost is Koran VII, 204–6. The mihrab arch bears Koran LIX, 23–4, the remaining space being filled with some of the '99 Names of God' which also, many in pairs, are crowded into the panelled spandrels. The panels of square Kufic in the upper corners bear the latter part of Koran XXI, 87. At the apex of the mihrab arch is a panel with praise of God and Muḥammad.

The field is a mihrab niche, springing rather high in the rectangle, with pointed horseshoe arch and consoles in the form of lobed half-medallions. The filling is a vertically symmetrical split-palmette spiral scroll overlying a dense spiral lotus-scroll very similar in drawing to the scrolling seen in *No. 32*. At the base is a lobed oval medallion with a smaller medallion at the centre and a filling of pomegranates. The border is a running scroll with notched stems and palmette- or lotus-heads, a coarser version of that of *No. 16*. The guard stripes are of double undulating lotus-scroll. The piece is damaged, doubtless from being stored while carelessly folded.

A recently published rug from the same group – without inscriptions and with borders arranged like those of the Yerkes carpet (cf. p. 27) but with the filling of the mihrab niche very comparable to the present piece – is in the Museo degli Argenti in Florence; cf. A. Boralevi, 'Three rugs in the Museo degli Argenti in Florence', *Halı* III/1 (1980), 48. No indication is given of the provenance of this rug, but there may well be archival evidence relating to its acquisition, which would do much to resolve the problems regarding the place and date of manufacture of this whole Palace group.

20 Prayer rug, warps and wefts yellow wool, Persian knot, 100 knots per square cm, pile wool enhanced with metal thread, Istanbul, or possibly Hereke, nineteenth century, in archaizing style; 13/2017. Dimensions 169 × 119 cm.
The three inscription borders are in grandly conceived rounded scripts. The outer inscription is the Āyat al-Kursī, Koran II, 255, and the following verse, complete; the main inscription, in four cartouches, two by two on each side, is Koran XXXIII, 56, while the broad panel above is the Shī'ī *shahāda*, with a number of rather elegant *fioriture*. The innermost inscription consists of praise of the Fourteen Immaculates. Of the two pairs of lobed medallions of square Kufic, none of them reversed, the upper pair are assorted *du'ā*: *subḥān[ahu] Allāh wa'l-ḥamdu li'llāh wa lā ilāh ilā'llāh*

wa Allāhu akbar, possibly with some otiose letters. The lower pair are composed of 'Muḥammad', repeated four times, with ''Alī', repeated four times, at the centre.
The field is designed as a mihrab niche with attenuated lobed arch filled with a decorated vase hanging *in vacuo* with chinoiserie lotus-trails issuing from it and cloud-bands below it. The lower part of the niche is filled with vertically symmetrical flowering Prunus trees and assorted flora at the base. At the very centre is a black patch with stylized flames, perhaps representing a fragment of the Ka'ba such as is enshrined in some of the sixteenth-century monuments of Istanbul (e.g. the mosque of Sokollu Meḥmed Paşa, inaugurated 1571). The main border has oblong cartouches with wriggling cloud-bands superimposed over floral scrolls with an 8-petalled rosette at each corner. The guard stripes are of floral scrolls in fainter versions of the 'International Timurid' chinoiserie style.

21 Prayer rug, warps yellow wool, wefts white cotton, Persian knot, 64 knots per square cm, pile wool, Istanbul, or possibly Hereke, nineteenth century, in archaizing style; 13/2033. Dimensions 169 × 119 cm.
The three inscription borders are all Koranic: the outermost XXVII, 30 + VI, 83–4 (as far as the word *Da'ūd*); the main inscription is the Āyat al-Kursī, II, 255, complete; the innermost XXIV, 35. The mihrab arch bears two complete Suras, CXII + CVIII. All the scripts are elegant and well arranged and show similarities to those of *No. 9*; they may, indeed, have been redrawn from the cartoons for that rug. The lobed medallions of square Kufic in the upper corners are of unidentified *ḥadīth*, the text, however, being as on *No. 10*.

The field is a mihrab niche with elegant lobed pointed arch, filled with a lobed ovoid medallion set on a decorated vase with an inverted crown at the base; this medallion is a more refined version of the one seen in *No. 12*. The ground is of rather angular flowering Prunus or fruiting pomegranate branches, comparable to those on *No. 10*. Above the medallion is a conspicuous panel with *Allāhu akbar kabīran/*'God is All-great, greatly'. The main border consists of cartouches filled with split-palmette scroll or stylized cloud-bands. The guard stripes are of undulating lotus- or floret-scrolls.

The colour-scheme is particularly remarkable among this group of Palace carpets for its lavish use of yellow.

22 Prayer rug, warps white wool, wefts ivory-coloured cotton thread, with some white cotton as well, Persian knot, 64 knots per square cm, pile wool, enhanced with metal thread, Istanbul, or possibly Hereke, nineteenth century, in archaizing style; 13/2025. Dimensions 150 × 115 cm.
Of the three inscription borders the outermost appears to be non-Koranic and in Persian. The principal inscription is the Āyat al-Kursī, Koran II, 255, complete, arranged in five narrow panels. The innermost, in quasi-*nasta'līq*, is Koran XVII, 78, complete. The mihrab arch bears an inscription, also in quasi-*nasta'līq*, Koran XIV, 40–1 + *ṣadaqa Allāh*. In the mihrab arch is a prominent panel with *Allāhu akbar kabīran/*'God is All-great, greatly'.

The field is a mihrab niche with pointed horseshoe arch and a tiny finial, with inside it a large medallion on an inverted crown and also having a small finial, and with a filling of a counterpoint of split-palmette arabesques and spiral lotus-scroll. The ground is a dense spiral scroll with scattered 'International Timurid', lotuses, peonies and leaves, doubtless drawn from the repertoire of the large sixteenth-century Uşak medallion carpets. The spandrels have heavily modelled split palmettes and similarly scattered chinoiserie lotuses and other blossoms. The medallion is a rather looser version of that seen on *No. 12*.

The confused main scrolling border is evidently copied, not particularly well, from the border of *No. 18*. The guard stripes are of undulating lotus- or peony-scroll.

23 Prayer rug, warps yellow wool at the top, then pink wool, wefts pink wool, Persian knot, 100 knots per square cm, pile wool, with considerable use of silver thread, Istanbul, or possibly Hereke, nineteenth century, in archaizing style; 13/2028. Dimensions 153 × 110 cm.
There are only two inscription borders, both Koranic: the principal one is the Āyat al-Kursī, II, 255, complete; the inner inscription, in quasi-*nastaʿlīq*, is XXXIII, 56. The two pairs of small rosettes with curiously arranged *naskhī* inscription filling bear praises to God.

The field is a mihrab niche with pointed lobed arch and a lobed contour, inside below and outside above. The filling is a vertically symmetrical split-palmette scroll overlying a dense spiral floral scroll with florets and bolder chinoiserie lotus-blossoms picked out in contrasting colours. The spandrels are bichrome with a few colour accents, of wriggling cloud-bands and spiral scroll. The main border consists of elongated panels and lobed lozenges filled with spiral scrolling overlaid with wriggling cloud-bands or filled with palmettes on a ground of fine floral scrollwork. The guard stripes are of undulating chinoiserie peony- or lotus-scrolls.

24 Prayer rug, warps and wefts yellow wool, Persian knot, 81 knots per square cm, pile wool enhanced with metal thread, Istanbul, or possibly Hereke, nineteenth century, in archaizing style; at each end there is a flat-woven strip, 2 cm deep, with lines of unidentified verse; 13/2160. Dimensions 136 × 90 cm.
With only very minor differences, this piece is a copy of *No. 23*, though it is markedly smaller and the arrangement of the Āyat al-Kursī, Koran II, 255, in differently proportioned panels, has led to the elimination of the rosettes with doxologies in the upper corners, while the scrolling ground of the panels has had to be redrawn and the cloud-band fillings of the lower panels re-adapted. It may be that the cartoons for the present piece were redrawn to fit another commission. Alternatively, cartoons of different sizes were available to the weavers in the workshop, and they would have been expected to adapt the rest of the design to suit them.

The piece has suffered damage from being stored while carelessly folded.

25 Prayer rug, warps and wefts yellow wool, Persian knot, 100 knots per square cm, pile wool, enhanced with silver thread, Istanbul, or possibly Hereke, nineteenth century, in archaizing style; 13/2039. Dimensions 136 × 90 cm.
The borders, with their inscriptions and cloud-band filling, are identical in content and in disposition to those of *No. 24*, though the inscriptions, and certainly the drawing and arrangement of the inner inscription, Koran XXXIII, 56, are identical to those on *No. 23* as well. However, although here the filling of the field and the spandrels of the mihrab niche are broadly similar to both the preceding examples, the present piece is the most elaborately drawn and executed, with finely contoured split-palmette scrolls overlying a dense spiral scroll brilliantly set with florets, buds and chinoiserie floral motifs from the 'International Timurid' repertoire. We may guess that this piece was the original after which *No. 24* was woven and that, very probably, *No. 23* was an adaptation of the design to rather larger dimensions.

The rug has suffered damage on the right-hand side and also at the centre, the result of having been stored while carelessly folded.

26 Prayer rug, warps red wool, wefts deep café-au-lait wool, braided, Persian knot, 96 knots per square cm, pile wool, Istanbul, or possibly Hereke, probably nineteenth century, in archaizing style; 13/2010. Dimensions 143 × 78 cm.
The field is a mihrab niche with pointed lobed arch and palmette finial, and with conspicuous corner-pieces at the base. The filling is of intersecting floral scrolls with black and yellow split palmettes as an overlay. The spandrels have similar scrollwork, but without the split palmettes. The border is a thin undulating floral scroll with imbricated cloud-bands. The guard stripes are of undulating floral scrolls.

Above the niche is an elegantly written panel rhyming *bābrā-miḥrābrā*, but possibly rhyming prose rather than verse, in Persian, the import of which is that if you wish for the door to be opened (i.e. to receive illumination), you should frequent the mihrab (i.e. retreat into prayer). This is evidently a reminiscence of Koran III, 37.

The design shows similarities to that of *No. 2*, as well as to eighteenth-century rugs from Bergama and Uşak. Somewhat comparable also is a rug 'from the tomb of Sultan Selīm (1885)' which at the time Ernst Kühnel (*Die Sammlung Türkischer und Islamischer Kunst im Tschinili Köschk*, Plate 37) published it (1938) was in the Çinili Köşk. The present location of that rug is unclear, since some pieces published in Kühnel's album are now in the Topkapı Saray collections, while others are in the Museum of Turkish and Islamic Art in Istanbul.

The piece is very worn and shows numerous transverse splits.

27 Prayer rug, warps undyed wool, wefts blue wool, Persian knot, 64 knots per square cm, pile wool, Istanbul, or possibly Hereke, nineteenth century, in archaizing style; 13/2041. Dimensions 145 × 102 cm.

The field is a mihrab niche with a pointed lobed arch and palmette finial, and with heavy lobed consoles in lieu of side columns. The filling is of ragged split palmettes, vertically symmetrical, over lax spiral scrolls with chinoiserie lotuses and pomegranates. The scrolls continue into the spandrels, which have heavy half-clips of cloud-bands. Above the mihrab is a panel of unidentified *ḥadīth*: *Qāl 'alayhi al-salām, Man ṣalla al-burdayn*(?) *dakhala al-jannat* [sic]/'The Prophet has said, "Who prays ... (*or* who utters a particular prayer) in retreat [cf. Persian, *bardīdan*] shall enter paradise."' The scrolling borders are overlaid with cloud-bands featuring frilly tips.

In its design and colour-scheme this piece is reminiscent of the famous small sixteenth-century Uşak rug in the Islamisches Museum, East Berlin (No. 1.24); cf. Kurt Erdmann, 'The discovery of the antique carpet' in *Seven Hundred Years of Oriental Carpets*, ed. Hanna Erdmann (London 1970), 27–8.

28   Prayer rug, warps undyed wool, wefts deep-blue wool, Persian knot, 64 knots per square cm, pile wool, possibly Cairo, probably nineteenth century, in archaizing style; 13/2015. Dimensions 133 × 96 cm.
The field is a mihrab niche with small angular pointed arch and a filling of lattice work of stiff half-palmettes and stylized lotus-heads. In the spandrels of the arch is *Allāhu: akbar*/'God is All-great', with 2-line panels to either side bearing the Shī'ī *shahāda*, *Lā ilāh ilā'llāh, Muḥammad rasūl Allāh, 'Alī walī Allāh ḥaqqan ḥaqqan*/'There is no god but God, Muḥammad is God's Prophet, 'Alī is the friend of God, in truth, in truth' – all in unpretentious *naskhī*. Above the arch is a panel of *naskhī du'ā*: *'ajjalū ṣalwat qabl al-fawt wa 'ajjalū bi'l-tawbat qabl al-mawt*/'Hasten to prayer before you pass (away) and hasten to repentance before death'. In either corner are small panels of square Kufic, that on the right being '*Allāh, Muḥammad, 'Alī*', that on the left being the name '*Alī*', four times repeated. At the apex of the mihrab arch is a lozenge also of square Kufic, also with '*Allāh, Muḥammad, 'Alī*'. Such inscriptions, outside the context of the Shī'ī *shahāda*, would not necessarily, however, have been Shī'ī in tenor.

The border is of scrolling chinoiserie lotuses with hollow palmettes, the motifs being woven in contrasting colours. The double guard stripes are of schematic floral scrolls.

The piece has suffered damage from being stored while carelessly folded.

29   Prayer rug, warps brick (red) wool, wefts green wool, Persian knot, 49 knots per square cm, pile wool, possibly Cairo, nineteenth century, in archaizing style; 13/2024. Dimensions 149 × 104 cm.
The field is a mihrab niche with small angular pointed arch, filled with a lattice of lozenges or cross-motifs of half-palmettes or lotus-heads, and having a bold octagon at the centre filled with a rosette and surrounded by cell-work strongly recalling the plan of a shrine and ambulatory, though which particular Muslim shrine is not evident. The cells are filled with florets and miniature stylized cypresses. The intention may be to represent Kerbela or Najaf.

The mihrab arch is filled with the names '*Umar, 'Alī, 'Uthmān*, surmounted by *Abū Bakr*, poorly written and arranged, and to either side are panels each made up of the name '*Alī*, four times repeated (the well-known Persian *chahār 'Alī* motif). Above the mihrab niche is the Shī'ī *shahāda*: *Lā ilāh ilā'llāh, Muḥammad rasūl Allāh, 'Alī walī Allāh ḥaqqan ḥaqqan*/'There is no god but God, Muḥammad is God's Prophet, 'Alī is the friend of God, in truth, in truth'. In the corners are small panels with the names *Allāh, Muḥammad, 'Alī*, in rather squashed rounded script, in which the *shāddas* are exaggerated and almost create confusion with '*Allāh*'. The border is an angular undulating scroll of highly stylized chinoiserie lotuses and half-palmettes. The guard stripes are of rosettes.

30   Prayer rug, warps undyed wool, wefts white double-spun wool, Turkish knot, 30 knots per square cm, pile wool, possibly Cairo, probably nineteenth century, in traditional style; 13/2026. Dimensions 150 × 109 cm.
The field is a mihrab niche with small angular pointed arch, filled with a lozenge grid of palmettes in a counterchange or reciprocal pattern. Above the mihrab niche is the Sunnī *shahāda*. The border is an angular undulating scroll with broken cloud-bands very highly stylized. The guard stripes are lotus bands, a motif evidently drawn from the repertoire of Cairene 'Mamlūk' rugs.

While the design is strongly reminiscent of the Anatolian 'Lotto' carpets, some features have suggested to recent commentators that, like *Nos. 28* and *29*, the group may not have been woven in Istanbul for the Palace but in a provincial centre, which might then suggest Cairo. The simple colour-schemes and the simplified patterns may, of course, suggest that the rugs were not woven for the Palace at all.

The piece has suffered damage from being stored while carelessly folded.

31   Prayer rug, warps deep-blue wool, wefts green wool, Persian knot, 120 knots per square cm, pile wool. The long fringe and the unworn state of the piece show that it was to be hung on a wall; the provenance is obscure, but it has been conjectured that the rug was a Palace order, possibly executed in Istanbul in the eighteenth century; 13/2014. Dimensions 100 × 75 cm.
The field is a mihrab niche with pointed lobed arch and a small finial, having a central lobed pointed medallion that rests upon a decorated vase and is surmounted by an almond-shaped inscription panel. The fillings of both spandrels and niche are roughly similar, with bichrome split palmettes and stylized chinoiserie lotuses, but are differentiated in colour. Above the niche is a carefully pointed panel of rounded script relating to prayer and to the place of prayer (*muṣallā*). The border is of alternating cartouches and lozenges with interlaces as filling, on a ground of continuous foliate trails. The guard stripes are also of cartouches, alternating with knot patterns, with repeated inscriptions: *Mubārak bād, sa'ādat bād, dawlat bād*, which occur frequently in seventeenth-century Ottoman epigraphy on decorative objects made for

the Sultans, and which are to be construed as prayers for the ruler's happiness, good fortune or blessed state. Those above and below are arranged so that they all read the right way up.

The decorative repertoire is much indebted to the designs of Uşak carpets, particularly those dated or datable to the eighteenth century.

The piece was published by Celâl Esad Arseven – cf. *Les Arts décoratifs turcs* (Istanbul n.d. [1952]), Fig. 635 – as 'eighteenth-century, Istanbul', but without corroboration.

32 Prayer rug, warps and wefts white cotton, Persian knot, 64 knots per square cm, pile wool in three colours only, Istanbul, or possibly Hereke, nineteenth century, in archaizing style; 13/2158. Dimensions 161 × 113 cm.
The border bears discrete panels of Persian *nasta'līq*, only intermittently decipherable and not attributable, the general import of which, however, seems to be that intimate discourse with God while praying is better than conventional prayer. The inscription on the mihrab arch is Koran XIV, 40–1.

The field is a mihrab niche with constricted pointed horseshoe arch, filled with a hanging decorated vase and with dense well-drawn scrollwork, heavily spiralling, with chinoiserie lotuses and peonies, feathery leaves and knotted cloud-bands, and a rather laxer scroll with similar motifs but with coiled split palmettes too in the spandrels. That part of the border not occupied by inscriptions is of dense spiral scrolls with split palmettes and other floral motifs. At the apex of the mihrab arch is *Allāhu akbar*/'God is All-great'.

While the Persian inscriptions on this group of carpets, if Shī'ī in tenor, are not markedly Sufi, the present piece seems to tend towards assertion of the individual will, a practice which would have been regarded by the *'ulamā'* as reprehensible. Unfortunately, however, examples of such inscribed carpets, even in Iran, are far too few to arrive at a more general conclusion on the religious status of the piece.

33 Prayer rug, warps and wefts white wool, Persian knot, 48 knots per square cm, pile wool, Istanbul, or possibly Hereke, nineteenth century, in archaizing style; 13/2044. Dimensions 157 × 119 cm.
The three inscription borders are very similar in appearance to those of *No. 20*, and the main inscription is identical in script. The outer band is of blessings upon the Fourteen Shī'ī Immaculates; the main inscription bears the Shī'ī *shahāda* at the head, with panels of square Kufic at the corners and Koran XXXIII, 56, in two panels at the sides. The innermost inscription is Koran II, 255, complete. At the apex of the mihrab arch and in the spandrels are 'Muḥammad, Allāh, 'Alī' (in that order, reading from right to left). The lobed panels of square Kufic are of assorted *du'ā*, neither being reversed: *subḥān[ahu] Allāh wa'l-ḥamdu li'llāh wa lā ilāh ilā'llāh wa Allāhu akbar*, possibly with some otiose letters. These formulae, which appear to be chosen haphazardly, must have been selected because their letter forms suited them particularly well for distortion into such panels of square Kufic.

The field is a mihrab niche with pointed lobed arch and prominent lobed consoles, filled with three hanging jar-like

lamps on a ground of symmetrically disposed spiralling scrolls overlaid by slender split palmettes. The spandrels have spiral scrolling and cloud-bands. The main border, a somewhat simplified version of that of *No. 20*, is of rosettes and elongated panels with cloud-bands or lotuses on a slender blossom-scroll. The guard stripes are of lotus- or split-palmette scroll.

34 Prayer rug, warps yellow wool, wefts green wool, Persian knot, 100 knots per square cm, pile wool enhanced with metal thread, Istanbul, or possibly Hereke, nineteenth century, in archaizing style; 13/2011. Dimensions 173 × 112 cm.
The three border inscriptions are all Koranic: the outermost is XXVII, 30 + VI, 83–4; the principal inscription is II, 255, complete; the inner inscription is XXIV, 35. The scripts and the disposition of the inscriptions are very similar to those of *No. 21*, but the cartoons for them seem to have been somewhat modified. The mihrab arch is also practically identical and similarly bears two whole Koranic Suras, CXII and CVIII. At the apex of the niche is *Allāhu akbar kabīran*/'God is All-great, greatly'. The panels of square Kufic at the upper corners are also similar to those on *No. 20*.

The field is a mihrab niche with a rather diminutive lobed pointed arch; within it a conspicuously decorated hanging ornament with tassels and decorative panelled decoration is overlaid by fine polychrome chinoiserie floral scrolls. The spandrels have arabesques overlying a dense spiral floral scroll, very similar to the decoration of *No. 21*. The cartouche border is also a finer version of that of *No. 21*, which was evidently woven using the present piece as its model. The guard stripes are of undulating chinoiserie floral scrollwork, in 'International Timurid' style. The design is particularly successful: its differences from *No. 21*, the adaptation, show that the weavers could re-use motifs without necessarily reproducing a whole design, and simplify whatever was beyond their competence.

35 Prayer rug, warps and wefts yellow wool, Persian knot, 100 knots per square cm, pile wool, enhanced with metal thread, Istanbul, or possibly Hereke, nineteenth century, in archaizing style; 13/2008. Dimensions 165 × 110 cm.
The three inscription borders are all Koranic: the outermost is II, 285–6; the main inscription II, 255, complete; and the innermost II, 256–7, incomplete. The outer and inner inscription are in a sort of quasi-*nasta'līq* script, while that around the mihrab arch, Koran XIV, 40–1, is even closer to *nasta'līq* in appearance. At the apex of the niche is an almond-shaped medallion bearing praises of God, as on *No. 14*. The panels of square Kufic all bear the latter part of Koran XI, 88.

The field is a mihrab niche with a narrow pointed lobed arch and a palmette finial with dense polychrome chinoiserie scrollwork overlaid by cloud-bands. The vertically symmetrical design is a denser version of the field of *No. 18*, though the similarities are perhaps less evident than the differences. The spandrels are of spiral floral scrolls on a sky-blue ground. The border, with alternating cartouches and rosettes, the former with cloud-bands overlying chinoiserie floral scrolls, is a finer version of the border of *No. 14*, which may well have been a copy of it. The guard bands are of undulating scrollwork with chinoiserie flowers from the 'International Timurid' repertoire.

36 Fragment from a large carpet (detail), warps and wefts white cotton, Turkish knot, 25 knots per square cm, pile wool, Anatolia, eighteenth century, probably Uşak; 13/2034. Dimensions 157 × 87 cm.
The field appears to have been a checked design with alternating floral elements – irises, lilies, narcissi etc., some spreading, some ascendant. The border is also composed of floral elements – alternating stylized Prunus branches and cypresses, with slenderer Prunus branches between and smaller flowers on the ground. The design is very comparable to that of tree rugs associated with Isfahan in the early seventeenth century, and may well derive from them. Cf. M. Dimand and Jean Mailey, *Oriental rugs in the Metropolitan Museum of Art*, op. cit., Figs. 111–12.

37 Prayer rug, warps and wefts ivory-coloured cotton, Turkish knot, 16 knots per square cm, pile wool, Anatolia, nineteenth century, Kayseri, with Gördes elements; 13/2236 (A.11677). Dimensions 144 × 113 cm.
The field is a mihrab niche with a pointed arch stepped in profile and edged with stylized blossoms. The two columns with palmette capitals and bases have a filling of lozenges. The arch is filled with motifs suggesting a hanging ornament. The spandrels have stylized branches with a panel of highly stylized pseudo-script above. The border is an undulating scroll with rosettes, lotus-heads and stylized feathery leaves suggesting some familiarity with the borders of Ottoman Court carpets woven in Cairo in the late-sixteenth and early-seventeenth centuries. The guard bands are of floral scroll.

38 Prayer rug, warps wool (of three different colours – undyed café-au-lait, then red and blue), wefts café-au-lait wool, Turkish knot, 12 knots per square cm, pile wool, Eastern Anatolia, nineteenth century, with Kazak features; 13/2249 (A.11690). Dimensions 157 × 114 cm.
The field is a mihrab niche with angular pointed arch and a filling of large medallions, rosettes and small palmettes in chains. The border is an angular undulating band with anchor-like motifs. The guard stripes are of chevron bands.
☐ For a very similar piece, cf. Ian Bennett (ed.), *Rugs and carpets of the world* (London 1977), 148 ('Sevan Kazak').

39 Prayer rug, warps red wool, wefts cream wool, Turkish knot, 12 knots per square cm, pile wool, Kırşehir-Mucur type, eighteenth or nineteenth century; 13/2265 (A.11706). Dimensions 120 × 95 cm.
The field is a mihrab niche with angular pointed arch, its inner edge having hook-like projections, and with a floral finial. The filling is of confronted motifs arranged diagonally. A rectangular panel at the base and also the spandrels of the arch are filled with bold four-petalled rosettes. The border is

an angular undulating scroll with stylized palmettes. The guard stripes are of florets or simple floral scrolls.

40 Prayer rug, warps deep-pink wool, wefts white wool, Turkish knot, 36 knots per square cm, pile wool, Bergama, seventeenth century; 13/2043. Dimensions 192 × 125 cm.
The field is a mihrab niche with pointed angular arch and at the bottom a re-entrant filled with an octagon. The niche is filled with confronted minbar-like triangles and a series of hanging ornaments, the central one being a stylized candelabrum but the side ornaments having tassels, suggesting the appearance of talismans or phylacteries. The octagon filling the re-entrant also has a tassel; the central motif is flanked by stylized candlesticks. The spandrels of the mihrab arch, which has a curious chimney-like finial, are filled with angular motifs recalling the re-entrant below. The border is of openwork triangular motifs deriving from the pseudo-Kufic borders of large- and small-pattern 'Holbein' or 'Lotto' rugs of the fifteenth–sixteenth centuries.
It is conceivable that the choice of motifs was influenced by Anatolian rugs ordered for synagogues. Otherwise, the bold motifs and the colour contrasts of the spandrels recall much earlier Anatolian wares, notably the group of 'Seljuk' carpets.
☐ Published in Celâl Esad Arseven, *Les arts décoratifs turcs* (Istanbul n.d. [1952]), Fig. 634.

41 Prayer rug (detail), flat-weave, warps and wefts wool, Anatolia, eighteenth century, specially commissioned; 13/1540. Dimensions 170 × 100 cm overall.
The field is a mihrab niche featuring a pointed arch with a partially stepped profile, and side columns reduced to hooked borders. At the apex of the niche is a stylized candelabrum. The spandrels are filled with a lattice of rosettes. The conspicuous border is a broken scroll of stylized lotuses and spotted tulips. The guard stripes are of angular repeating motifs or rosettes. Though not at all comparable in appearance to the recently discovered and identified Court kilims from the Great Mosque at Divriği and other Anatolian sites, the present kilim is of high quality and indicates that pieces were on occasion specially commissioned from village looms for the bourgeoisie and high officials in Istanbul.

42 Kilim (detail), slit tapestry weave, wool, woven as two narrow strips which have then been sewn together, Central Anatolia, nineteenth century; 13/2157. Purchased 1972. Dimensions 270 × 140 cm overall.

43 Kilim (detail), wool, slit tapestry weave, woven as two narrow strips which have then been sewn together, Eastern Anatolia, nineteenth century (Afshar nomad); 13/2261 (A.11702). Dimensions 331 × 118 cm overall.

44, 45 Kilims (details), wool, slit tapestry weave, each made as two narrow strips and sewn together, Eastern Anatolia, nineteenth century (Afshar nomad); 13/2263 and 13/2264 (A.11704 and A.11705). Dimensions 336 × 154 cm and 200 × 154 cm overall, respectively.

4

Historic Persian carpets in the
Topkapı Saray collections

IT must appear somewhat ironic, in view of the traditional Western association of Iran with the fine pile carpet, that the only Persian carpet of any antiquity illustrated in the present volume (*No. 58*) is a very worn fragment with panels of *nasta'līq* verses from the *Divan* of Ḥāfiẓ; this is one of a well-known group of carpets associated with Kashan or North-West Iran in the later sixteenth and the seventeenth centuries.[1] In itself this fragment is no evidence for Ottoman taste in Persian carpets, but independent evidence exists for the sixteenth century to bear out the impression conveyed by the Treasury inventories of the beginning of the century that the Persian carpets in the Topkapı Saray were comparatively few in number and were acquired as booty or tribute, rather than in response to Court orders. The reasons for this are extremely obscure, not least because we have very little idea of the appearance of Persian carpets made *c*.1500. Our knowledge of fifteenth-century types is conjectural and limited to representations of Persian carpets in miniatures, for the accuracy of which there is little or no guarantee.[2] It has been suggested, however, that up to 1500 or so the repeating designs on the carpets depicted in miniatures could have been reproduced from carpets with designs not dissimilar to Anatolian 'Holbein' patterns. *If* these 'Holbeins' were used in the Ottoman palaces (an important qualification, for we can only guess), their Persian equivalents may not, to Ottoman eyes, have been sufficiently different in appearance to justify the extra cost and risk in ordering them.

In North-West Iran the sixteenth century saw a revolution anyway in carpet design that was certainly as great as the revolutions in the design of Uşak and of Cairene carpets; monster carpets, evidently specially ordered for the Safavid Court at Tabriz, are typified by the Ardabil carpet, dated 946/1539–40, now in the Victoria and Albert Museum, London – though this is not to take any particular view as to where, for whom or for what purpose, or even when exactly it was woven. These carpets, with their often lavish flora and fantastic fauna, their minutely detailed designs for borders,

medallions and grounds and their rich colour-schemes which have made them classics of carpet design, are very deeply indebted to the miniaturizing approach to manuscript illumination at the Court of Shah Ṭahmāsp (1524–76), whose scriptorium, at least up to a crisis of confidence in the 1540s which led him to promulgate an 'Edict of Sincere Repentance' for his youthful patronage of the illustrated book and to dismiss several of his best artists, was the largest and most talented in the Islamic world.[3] The cartoons, which doubtless were not for whole carpets but for constituent elements of the overall design (such as borders, medallions and corner-pieces) which then could be shuffled and recombined to make new designs, were evidently not confined to a single Court workshop but circulated rather widely: carpets woven to these designs may therefore have been made at most of the large urban centres.

The existence of Court looms in the reign of Shah Ṭahmāsp, strictly to cater for the needs of the Court, is highly probable, given the vast dimensions of the surviving carpets, but the location of such looms is very unclear, for the greater part of Shah Ṭahmāsp's reign was marked by war with Ottoman Turkey, when Tabriz and much of Persian Azerbaijan, as well as some of Shirvan too, were regularly sacked and occupied – a situation which led him to transfer his capital in 1548 to the securer and more distant city of Qazvin. Some indication of the fact that the workshop was not at Tabriz or possibly not in North-West Iran at all is the absence of any mention in Ottoman Palace registers both of craftsmen from Tabriz and of sixteenth-century Ottoman carpets in Safavid Court style. Both Selīm I and Süleymān the Magnificent practised conscription of skilled craftsmen from the foreign cities they captured, and sent them back to work in Istanbul; and though the system cannot have worked as well as this bald statement may suggest, we should have expected Persian carpet-weavers to have been among the craftsmen conscripted from Tabriz. The weaving centre was thus presumably located some considerable distance from the theatre of war, though the extremely high quality of the surviving carpets argues for constant and strict central supervision of the work.

Some of the sixteenth-century carpets customarily attributed to North-West Iran display Anatolian features. These examples may have been commercial or provincial versions of the Court medallion carpets. Alternatively, they could have been adaptations of Anatolian small-pattern 'Holbeins' which possibly reached Tabriz.

The earliest known document suggesting that the great Safavid medallion carpets could have had an impact on Ottoman Court taste is a letter dated 963/1555-6 from Shah Ṭahmāsp to Süleyman the Magnificent, said to have been brought with the Safavid embassy to congratulate Süleymān on the inauguration of the mosque of Süleymaniye in Istanbul in 1557, though the date of the letter suggests that it may in fact have been written in connection with the earlier embassy to Amasya, in 1555-6, which negotiated a peace after more than twenty years of warfare:[4]

> The effort to embellish holy places is highly desirable and extremely laudable ... hence it would be quite commendable to make carpets for their decoration; it is, moreover, one of the essential things for the new mosque [Süleymaniye]. The carpets made in these dominions are not of bad value and this friend, too, knows a little of the art of painting. He regards it as proper to send carpets without hesitation, but ceremoniously for the use of the newly built mosque, that august place of worship ... The success of the work depends upon obtaining the exact measurements of the length and width, as well as determining the colour of the field and the border. If it is agreed that these details should be precisely recorded by means of an iron ruler, ascertaining length and width, they can be sent through Tibbat Āghā [the Safavid ambassador], the humblest of the slaves in the palace of 'The Refuge of the World'. By this means all danger of the carpets being too large or too small will be averted. In the same way measurements can be taken for the carpets [to be] spread on the floor of the mosque for the use of the congregation who offer their prayer of obedience standing on the threshhold of servitude and submission ...

Many of the peculiarities of this letter, which is cited in its translation by Ettinghausen and Minovi, as well as some of its obscurities, can be put down to the flowery locutions of Persian Chancery secretarial style. Shah Ṭahmāsp's (or his ambassador's) grand ideas on the proper way in which mosques should be decorated do not seem to have accorded with the original ideas for floor-coverings for Süleymaniye, the principal material ordered having been a large number of reed mats from Egypt (*burya-i Mıṣır*). The insistence on providing exact measurements, which cannot have been necessary for the drawing of cartoons, suggests rather that what was being offered was small carpets for the Imperial box (*ḥunkār maḥfili*), from which the Sultan would hear the Friday prayer, and where it would be necessary to specify dimensions. Alternatively, it may indicate a degree of proportionality in Safavid carpet design: thus, a stipulated length would imply a certain corresponding width, medallions of a particular size, etc. Such stipulations would be less important in the case of a cartoon for a complete carpet, but essential if cartoons for separate design elements were to be used together.

As with any fragmentary correspondence, we know neither the background to Shah Ṭahmāsp's proposal nor its precise results. At the peace of Amasya signed in 1556 the lavish presents from the Persian mission certainly included carpets[5] and even a less ceremonious embassy in 1561 offered carpets too.[6] If the proposal evoked explicit agreement from the Ottoman side and the requested information was sent by return, it would still have taken several years for the commissions to be executed. Estimates of the time necessary have varied, but we do not have to assume that this would have been regarded as an urgent commission. This makes it highly likely, therefore, that the carpets brought late in 1566 by the Safavid embassy to congratulate Selīm II on his accession were either the carpets woven to order, or something very like them. These gifts are known both from the diary of Archbishop Antonius Verantius (Vrančić),[7] a Habsburg emissary, from the chronicler Selāniki and from a work by Seyyid Loqmān, Murād III's official chronicler, the *Şahanşāhnāme* (Istanbul University Library, F.1404) completed in 989/1581-2, folios 41b–42a of which show the embassy staggering under the weight of its offerings. These included wall-hangings from Darabjird (possibly *Dārāī*/'fit for Darius', thus a description rather than a provenance) and silk carpets from Hamadan and Darguzin, twenty large and many small, with birds, animals and flowers brocaded in gold; nine camel-hair (possibly camlet, i.e. mohair) carpets; and fine woollen (*tiftīk*) carpets so large that *seven men could scarcely carry one of them*. These last must have been the great floor carpets such as Shah Ṭahmāsp proposed for the congregation at Süleymaniye. Unfortunately there is no surviving trace of them.

It has often been suggested that the large Uşak medallion carpets of the same period woven to Court order owed their design to Persian models, but Julian Raby's demonstration that on the contrary (see p. 12) these Uşaks owe their designs to Ottoman binding stamps renders this suggestion less plausible, though there may have been some general indebtedness. However, the 1566 embassy set a fashion in Safavid gifts which did much to create a taste at the Ottoman Court for fine Persian carpets.

A recent account, based on unpublished manuscript sources, of the Sūr-i Humāyūn, the elaborate festivities held on the Hippodrome in Istanbul in 1582 to celebrate the Circumcision of the sons of Murād III (the elder being the crown prince, Şehzāde Meḥmed, later Meḥmed III), shows the trend continuing.[8] The presents offered by the various foreign embassies are roughly classifiable geographically: wolf- or deer-hounds, velvets and other silks, furs, silver and goldsmiths' work from the ambassadors of Venice, Ragusa, Transylvania, Poland, etc. (plate from Ragusa and Transylvania was particularly popular at the Ottoman Court); slaves and concubines from the Crimea; talismans against the plague, sables and theriac from the Uzbek Khan 'Abd-allāh in Bukhara; incense, ambergris, aloes wood, a precious jewelled flask of Zemzem water and part of the Ka'ba covering from the Sharif of Mecca; and silks, velvets and brocades richly worked with metal thread, sashes, cloths, overgarments, belts and armbands, gems, porcelains, saddlery, weapons, precious Korans by the most famous calligraphers and richly illuminated and illustrated manuscripts of the Persian classics, falcons, fine horses, spices, scents and rare drugs – in short the whole trappings of diplomatic gifts – from the Safavid Shah Muḥammad Khudābende, his son, Mīrzā Ḥamza, his daughter and their ambassador Ibrāhīm Khān to Murād III, Şehzāde Meḥmed, Mūrad III's mother and even to his harem. The lavishness of the Persian gifts, particularly in comparison with those from European powers and from other Muslim rulers, may be explained partly by the physical proximity of the two states, partly by the war between Turkey and Iran which had broken out in 1577. Although costly and inconclusive for the Ottomans, the war had on balance been more disastrous for the Safavids in terms of territory occupied and cities devastated. The festivities of the Sūr-i Humāyūn provided a convenient opportunity, there-fore, to send a mission to sue for an armistice.

The listing of presents by source on the basis of geography may nevertheless give a misleading idea of their ulterior provenance, for it is somewhat anachron-istic to judge embassies of the period and their gifts by comparison with the modern diplomatic practice of making official gifts serve as a showcase for national arts and industries. Indeed, in the sixteenth and seventeenth centuries it was not nationalism but, convenience or expense – or, rather exceptionally, concern for what would be most acceptable – which dictated the choice of gifts; this meant that one bought where one could or as cheaply as was consonant with putting on a show of

magnificence, and as far as possible took the opportun-ity to recycle unwanted gifts received from other embassies. The rulers of Fez and Marrakesh, for example, sent not only a precious rosary in a casket inlaid with mother-of-pearl, a turban-ornament with osprey feathers and jewelled pin, saddlery damascened, jewelled and sewn with pearls, silks, brocades and cloth of gold, but in addition two prayer rugs worked with metal thread and four silk prayer rugs that included flowering and fruiting branches in their designs. It would, however, be dangerous to regard this gift of prayer rugs as evidence for fine carpet-weaving in Morocco at this time; and indeed the only other carpets presented on the occasion of the Sūr-i Humāyūn were those offered by the Safavid embassy: 'incomparable' carpets, some from Yazd and some from Khurasan, to Murād III; two pairs of silk prayer rugs, as brilliantly decorated as they were fine, to Murād III's mother; and two prayer rugs brocaded with metal thread to Şehzāde Meḥmed. Though in comparison with the other gifts, notably the jewellery and the precious Korans, these carpets occupy a minor place, and since no carpets were offered by the viziers or the other ambassadors and guests, one must conclude that such carpets were still great rarities at the Ottoman Court in the late sixteenth century and that, very probably, the Moroccan gifts were Persian in provenance too. It is, of course, scarcely surprising that the embassies from the European powers offered no carpets – an idea which must have seemed like carrying coals to Newcastle, if they gave the matter so much thought – but this shows the Safavid gifts in even greater prominence.

The role of royal gifts in establishing a taste for Persian carpets at the Ottoman Court was all the more necessary because of the frequent interruptions to Ottoman–Safavid trade in the wars of the sixteenth century, by embargo as well as by confiscation or loot. Embargoes were officially used as an instrument of Ottoman policy from the reign of Selīm I (1512–20) onwards and appear at least temporarily to have been remarkably efficiently enforced.[9] The aspect of inter-national trade most affected was the supply of raw silk from Shirvan, Gilan and Mazandaran, most of which was re-exported to Italy and France via Bursa or Aleppo, though some of it may have been used in the Ottoman silk industry. The penalties for infraction, of which confiscation or heavy fines were the least severe, for a time brought the caravan trade across Anatolia to a halt and, although the Black Sea route to Trebizond and Tabriz was used by some European travellers, the trade seems largely to have been diverted south via Basra or Baghdad and up the Euphrates to Aleppo. Aleppo also presented risks, however, for it was a large Ottoman garrison city (which Süleymān often visited), as well as being the great commercial centre of the Near East with Venetian and French factories, and the letters of Andrea Berengo[10] in the mid-sixteenth century frequently complain of the scarcity and exorbitant cost of the Persian raw silk which did succeed in arriving on the Aleppo market. And although it is difficult to arrive at quantitative estimates, the maritime ascendancy of the Portuguese in the Indian Ocean and their development of the port of Hormuz on the Gulf must further have exacerbated the shortages by encouraging the export of raw silk by the direct sea route to Northern Europe. It is not surprising at all, therefore, that the diffusion of luxury goods from Persia in Ottoman Turkey should have been largely confined to diplomatic gifts: there is, indeed, not a single document so far published relating to the availability or acquisition of any Persian textile on the market in sixteenth-century Ottoman Turkey.

To some, incalculable, extent, obviously, this absence of Persian wares must have resulted from local taste. Why go after Persian silks when the velvets, brocades and cloth of gold of Florence and Venice, as well as from the looms of Bursa and Istanbul, were so freely available? And why go after Persian carpets when those from Anatolia were of such good quality? But, equally, the absence or virtual absence of Persian manufactures from the Istanbul market was no stimulus to a change in taste.

For much of the sixteenth century the Safavids reacted passively to these Ottoman embargoes and seizures of contraband silk, but under the actively anti-Ottoman policy of Shah 'Abbās I (1587–1629), whose European diplomacy was devoted to the stifling of trade with Ottoman Turkey by further development of the direct sea route for transporting goods in Portuguese and then increasingly English and Dutch vessels[11] and by increasing use of the overland route through the Caucasus or across the Caspian and then up the Volga to North Russia and thence to Poland and the Baltic. Shah 'Abbās's transfer of the Safavid capital from Qazvin to Isfahan in 1597–8 was associated with the creation of all sorts of Court workshops there and, although it seems that the finest silk-pile and tapestry-weave rugs continued to be made at Kashan (some 140 km north of Isfahan), the location of the manufacturing centres, like the diverted trade routes, meant that new design trends in the finest Persian carpets became yet more inaccessible to the Ottoman market, for they were sent by sea direct to Europe.

It was in these circumstances that the finest products of the Persian looms began to reach Europe in the early-seventeenth century, for example via Safavid embassies to Venice in 1603 and 1622,[12] which presented silk Polonaise carpets, some of which, now deplorably worn, are still in the Treasury of St Mark's Basilica. Moreover, largely through the intermediacy of Armenian merchants and factors in Łwów[13] with connections in Isfahan, silk-pile and tapestry-weave carpets, some brocaded with silver and gold thread, were ordered for European monarchs. These included the silk tapestry rug, now in the Residenzmuseum in Munich, bearing the arms of the Vasa kings of Poland – a piece which may be one of those featuring the Polish arms which are known to have been ordered and executed at Kashan in 1602.[14] The extent to which these luxurious Polonaise carpets and even more luxurious tapestry weaves ousted fine Turkish carpets from the European market is unclear, but they were evidently exported to Northern Europe in considerable numbers in the seventeenth century and became indispensable furnishings for the palaces and great houses of the Baroque era.

Shah 'Abbās's commercial policy was brilliant as an idea, but he lacked the means and the organization to be able to implement it with sufficient rigour to bring trade with the Ottomans to a halt, and the policy was tacitly abandoned by his successors. For already in the reign of Shah 'Abbās we find evidence that Persian carpets were available on the market in Istanbul. One such must have been the medallion and animal carpet belonging to Prince Roman Sanguszko, which is said to have been captured at the battle of Chocim (Hotin) in 1621 and which gives its name to that particular group of carpet designs.[15] And there is a very interesting letter, dated 19 March 1639, from the agent of Prince George I Rákóczi, prince of Transylvania, describing a large and expensive silk Persian carpet which he had found for him. Writing from Istanbul, he states:[16]

> Your Excellency, I have found very beautiful Persian rugs in one place. The length of these is five cubits and the width three cubits. Some are four and a half cubits long and two cubits and two quarters' [Hungarian *fertály*, some way after the German *Viertel*, a fraction of the Ottoman cubit/*dhirā'* described as a 'quarter'/*rubu'*, though quite often a cubit may have more than six 'quarters']. These cost 50, 60 or 70 Thalers each. There is one among them, Your Excellency, that is woven with gold and silver threads. I have never seen such a rug. It is three cubits and one 'quarter' long and two cubits and one 'quarter' wide and is a marvel to behold. It depicts two pairs of confronted peacocks, or rather pelicans; their faces are worked in gold and silver threads. Above their heads is a large handsome flower; even the fringes contain some silver thread. Its price is 125 Thalers.

Since Persian rugs with silk pile and metal thread were evidently still the prerogative of the Ottoman

Court, the carpet described must have been quite a find. It is, indeed, quite probable that even in the seventeenth century Istanbul was not a major entrepôt for Persian carpets at all, for what the Safavid commercial policies had failed to achieve had been accomplished by the Celali uprisings which from 1550 onwards had been a danger to trade from the East across Anatolia and which reached a peak of disruption in the early seventeenth century. Tamás Borsos's description of the reception of a Persian embassy in Istanbul in 1619, which offered 'beautiful and costly silk rugs' with brocading and metal thread, though some were simpler, still seems a typical explanation for the appearance of such pieces in Istanbul.[17]

On the Transylvanian side there is further evidence of Persian carpets on the local market and Albert Eichhorn[18] has produced interesting records of 'Persian' carpets listed in customs documents: (for the moment, abandoning the inverted commas) Persian carpets with a white ground; Persian carpets with red columns; Persian carpets with red flowers; red Persian carpets of novel design; crimson table Persian carpets; fine white Persian carpets; blue Persian carpets; yellow Persian carpets; floral Persian carpets; a Persian carpet with a blue central medallion; and a Persian carpet with arrows(?) at the centre. It is more than possible that the attribution 'Persian' is misleading and that some of the carpets, if not all, are Anatolian. Nevertheless, the mere grouping 'Persian' conveys an awareness that in Istanbul there were some genuine Persian carpets to be had by the fortunate few, and, doubtless, 'Persian' carpets by the gullible.

Kurt Erdmann, in his important studies on Oriental carpets in Italy, remarked that, frustratingly, the provenance of the large number of major Persian carpets which left the great houses and churches of Italy for museum collections in Europe and the United States in the late-nineteenth and the early-twentieth centuries cannot in any case be traced further back than about 1850. It seems likely that many of these came via Ottoman Turkey, but sometimes at an interval of several generations and very probably via the trade, as well as through diplomatic gifts. It may be that a great deal of work in Italian archives would do something to remedy the neglect of which Erdmann complained, but a more fruitful source might be the inventories of European *Türkenbeute*, from the Relief of Vienna in 1683 and the subsequent European victories in Central and Eastern Europe.

These have been the subject of a pioneering article by Kurt Erdmann[19] in which he concluded that all the carpets said to have been acquired at the siege of Vienna are in fact Persian. Among the carpets with such attributions are: booty associated with John Sobieski, a Polonaise in the church of St John in Studziana and three Polonaises (now destroyed) formerly in Frauenburg cathedral; and, possibly, a large white-ground animal carpet, half of which is in the sacristy of Kraków cathedral and the other half in the Musée des Arts Décoratifs in Paris, though its acquisition may date as much as a century before the Relief of Vienna. Other carpets, including one in the Landesmuseum, Karlsruhe, and a carpet from the royal house of Saxony, now in the Metropolitan Museum of Art, New York, are thought to have been booty from the campaigns, mostly post-1683, in which the Markgraf Ludwig Wilhelm of Baden (1655–1707), known as 'Türkenlouis', took part, and to these may be added a yellow-ground medallion carpet also in the Metropolitan Museum, probably Tabriz, c.1600, and the Anhalt medallion carpet, also now in New York. There is a further carpet alleged to be from the Relief of Vienna: a Herat, or possibly a Mughal, piece which is sometimes said to be from Ḳara Muṣṭafā Paşa's tent[20] and which was then presented by Leopold I to the Church of the Nome di Maria, on the Forum in Rome, founded in 1683 to commemorate the Relief of Vienna.

The rather aberrant provenance of this last carpet brings up a problem in the attributions of such '*Türkenbeute*'. Such was the enthusiasm aroused by the Turkish defeat at Vienna that 'Turkish booty' became quite a vogue among European collectors and the term came to be used as a convenient general designation for Persian and Turkish objects, many of which had no real relevance to the campaign, while some other Oriental objects of no relevance whatsoever to it were cheerfully accepted as booty. There is, for example, a Japanese Momoyama mother-of-pearl and lacquer casket in Stift Altenburg in Lower Austria, which as a monastery, one might feel, had no business to be collecting *Türkenbeute* at all; this object is said, not altogether convincingly, to have been captured at the Relief of Vienna. It might well, therefore, be prudent to take most attributions of carpets said to have been 'from the tent of Ḳara Muṣṭafā Paşa' with a large pinch of salt.

It is inconvenient to have to admit that our knowledge of the Habsburg collections of carpets, either Turkish or Persian, is very limited. There is a famous, and very important inventory of the Kunstkammer of Rudolf II, dated 1607–11,[21] and it would have been splendid if this had listed the carpets. These, however, must have been recorded in the inventory of tapestries and other furnishings, which — like those of the parade weapons and armour, as well as the regalia, and the paintings and the art gallery — have apparently not survived.

This said, Erdmann's decision to ignore carpets with alleged provenances from the Relief of Vienna but generally datable before 1650, on the grounds that Ḳara Muṣṭafā Paṣā would certainly have furnished his tent with carpets which were not antiques but new, is unconvincing because it takes no account either of the general custom of the Ottoman commissariat on campaign or of the peculiar circumstances of the 1683 campaign in particular. This venture was in fact a rather self-conscious exercise in refighting history, namely the campaign of Süleymān the Magnificent in 1529 which, but for the atrocious weather on the way which fatally delayed the advance, would almost certainly have culminated in the capture of Vienna. The chroniclers of Ḳara Muṣṭafā Paṣā's campaign and of the siege of Vienna lose no occasion to remark on the way in which Süleymān's tactics and even the positions he had occupied were later rehearsed, though how the writers expected such blind imitation of his movements to bring success is not altogether clear. The equipping of a vizier's army has long been recognized to be largely a matter of improvisation, for it would have been inordinately expensive to issue new equipment on each occasion. It was therefore standard practice to re-issue tents, armour and equipment, and sometimes even banners, from the Ottoman Armoury or the Imperial Stores. The great tents preserved in the Topkapı Saray and the Military Museum in Istanbul, in the Wawel in Kraków, in Ingolstadt and in London are a signal illustration of the way in which older tents were taken out of store, repaired and refurbished; this prudent policy must go back to the earliest days of the Ottoman Empire. The tent of the vizier, as the Sultan's representative on campaign, would of course have been more splendid than the rest, and its furnishings would have been in better condition. It would therefore have been more like the Imperial tent, described by Benaglia at Belgrade in 1682,[22] with a portable throne with baldaquin and silk bolsters on a dais spread with valuable Persian carpets.

This situation makes it *a priori* highly likely that the trappings and furnishings of Ḳara Muṣṭafā Paṣā's tent at Vienna, which fell into John Sobieski's hands at the relief of the city, were not by any means brand new. This seems to have been all the more the case in that conscious reminiscence of Süleymān the Magnificent's Vienna campaign of 1529 must have encouraged the Ottomans to take with them valued antiques. Sobieski's letter to his wife describing the extraordinary experience of entering the vizier's tent, which had been abandoned on the withdrawal of the Ottoman armies, does not in fact mention carpets at all,[23] but there were so many other treasures to catch his eye. The tent and its contents were then divided up among the troops in accordance with the law of spoils of war, and it is to this division that the carpets associated with Vienna now in the Wawel and in various Polish churches evidently owe their provenance.

However, the exotica subsequently associated with Ḳara Muṣṭafā Paṣā's Vienna campaign may well not all be fictitious attributions by European monarchs anxious to establish a claim to have been present at the defeat of the Ottomans. Recently in London there was exhibited, for example, a silk and metal-thread tent-hanging, of Moroccan or Tunisian manufacture, which is an exact replica of a panel now in the Wawel that is also believed to be booty from Vienna.[24] Until 1979 this textile had remained in the family of Prince John Oginski, Palatine of Polóck and Field Hetman of the Grand Duchy of Lithuania, who died early in 1684 at Kraków of wounds received at Vienna. These pieces also are unique and demonstrate further the degree of eclecticism, even improvisation, which governed the furnishing of the vizier's tent.

Although the history of Persian carpets at the Ottoman Court in the sixteenth and seventeenth centuries does not give reason to believe that the fashion for fine Persian carpets swept Turkey as it did Europe in the seventeenth and eighteenth centuries, it shows that they were appreciated at Court as luxuries, exotica and, sometimes, as exceptionally fine pieces of weaving, and that there was at least a limited market for such pieces in Istanbul. However, Istanbul at this time was not an important entrepôt for the Persian trade, while even on the European side it is unlikely that we shall ever have complete archival documentation of the import trade in Persian carpets sufficient to enable us to evaluate it relative to the carpet trade with Turkey. By the nineteenth century the position had changed. In response to European demand, mass-produced Persian carpets for a middle-class market were imported into Turkey *en masse* and could be obtained in Istanbul more readily and easily than by journeying either to Teheran or to any of the provincial Persian carpet-manufacturing centres.

It is to this market that the other Persian carpets illustrated in the present volume owe their origin. They were bequeathed to the Turkish State by a rich Lebanese, Misbah Muhayyeṣ, who had settled in Istanbul during the First World War. He acquired the first large hotel in Istanbul, the Pera Palace, which he renovated and furnished to a high standard with Oriental objects, many of which were antiques, making it into a virtual museum of late-nineteenth-century European Orientaliste taste. The carpets formerly adorned the bedrooms and public rooms of the hotel:

many of them appear to have been left in bond and were periodically brought out as other pieces wore out or when it was desired to refurnish a room. On the death of Misbah Muhayyeş in 1954, the carpets were collected, cleaned and underwent a long process of restoration, finally reaching the Topkapı Saray Museum in 1980. Most of these nineteenth-century carpets are Persian — Hamadans, Saruks, Isfahans, together with pieces from Kirman and Kirmanshah — but there are also some fine Caucasian pieces (mostly Shirvans), as well as some Turcoman carpets and a very few pieces from Anatolia. Though none of them are individually of great intrinsic importance, as a group they give an interesting picture of what was to be found on the market in Istanbul in the late nineteenth century and are thus a useful document for the more recent history of the carpet trade. Moreover, when the history of the Pera Palace comes to be written, they will be a valuable source for the impact of European Orientalism on the middle-class taste of late Ottoman Turkey.

NOTES TO CHAPTER 4

1   Kurt Erdmann, 'Verses on carpets' in *Seven Hundred Years of Oriental Carpets*, ed. Hanna Erdmann and trans. May H. Beattie and Hildegard Herzog (London 1970), 163–6.

2   A. Briggs, 'Timurid carpets. I. Geometric carpets', *Ars Islamica* VIII (1940), 20–54.

3   M. B. Dickson and S. C. Welch, *The Houghton Shahname* (Harvard University Press, Cambridge, Mass. 1981).

4   Text published in Ch. Schéfer, *Chrestomathie persane* II (Paris 1885), 220. For further references see J. M. Rogers, 'The State and the arts in Ottoman Turkey. 2. The furnishing and decoration of Süleymaniye', *International Journal of Middle East Studies* 14 (1982), 283–313.

5   J. von Hammer-Purgstall, *Geschichte des Osmanischen Reiches* (10 vols., Pest, 1827–35) III, 326.

6   Ibid., III, 391.

7   Quoted *in extenso*, ibid., III, 517–22.

8   Ibid., IV, 118–36; Orhan Şaik Gökyay, 'Bir sünnet düğünü', *Topkapı Sarayi Müzesi. Yıllık* I (1986), 21–55 (the sources the author has used are *Sūrnāme*, Topkapı Saray Library, H.1344; Loqmān, *Şahanşāhnāme*, Istanbul University Library, F.1404; Muṣṭafā 'Alī, *Cāmiʿ al-Buḥūr der Mecālis-i Sūr*, Topkapı Saray Library, B.203).

9   J.-L. Bacqué-Grammont, 'Etudes turco-safavides. I. Notes sur le blocus du commerce iranien par Sélim Iᵉʳ', *Turcica* VI (1978), 68–78.

10   Ugo Tucci, *Lettres d'un marchand vénitien Andrea Berengo (1553–1556)* (Paris 1956).

11   R. W. Ferrier, 'The European diplomacy of Shāh 'Abbās and the first Persian embassy to England', *Iran* XI (1975), 75–92.

12   C. Berchet, 'La repubblica di Venezia e la Persia', *Raccolta Veneta* I/1 (Venice, 1866), 5–62; Giovanni Curatola, 'Tessuti e artigianato turco nel mercato veneziano' in *Venezia e i Turchi* (Banca Cattolica del Veneto, 1985), 186–95.

13   Cf. *The Eastern carpet in the Western world*, exhibition catalogue (London 1983), 89–96; Friedrich Spuhler, 'Der figurale Kaschan-Wirkteppich aus der Sammlungen der regierenden Fürsten von Liechtenstein', *Kunst des Orients* V/1 (1968), 55–61.

14   *The Eastern carpet in the Western world* (op. cit.), No. 73; T. Mańkowski 'Note on the cost of Kashan carpets at the beginning of the seventeenth century', *Bulletin of the American Institute for Persian Art and Archaeology* VI (New York 1936), 152ff.

15   Hammer-Purgstall; op. cit. (note 5), IV, 526–8.

16   A. Beke and S. Barabás (eds.), *I Rákóczi György és a Porta. Levelekés okiratok* (George I Rákóczi and the Porte. Letters and documents) (Budapest 1888), 407–8; Veronika Gervers, *The influence of Ottoman Turkish textiles and costume in Eastern Europe* (Toronto 1982), 27.

17   T. Borsos, *Vásárhelytöl a Fényes Portáig: Emlékiratok levelek* (From Marosvásárhely/Tirgu Mureş to the Sublime Porte: Memoirs, letters), 2nd ed., L. Kocziany (Bucharest 1972), 279.

18   Albert Eichhorn, 'Kronstadt [i.e. Brassó, Braşov] und der orientalische Teppich', *Forschungen zur Volks- und Landeskunde* X (Bucharest 1967), 72–84; Ferenc Batári, in 'Turkish rugs in Hungary', *Halı* III/2 (1980), 82–90, adduces a wide variety of archival documents to show that 'Persian' carpets were also available in Hungary at this time.

19   Kurt Erdmann, 'Carpets as Turkish booty' in *Seven Hundred Years of Oriental Carpets*, op. cit. (note 1), 92–4. In the W. H. Moore collection there was also a Shah 'Abbās carpet with a label on the back, 'A. D. Wilkonski xii Septembris 1683 z pod Więdnia' Cf. Erdmann, ibid.

20   *Die Türken vor Wien. Europa und die Entscheidung der Donau 1683*, exhibition catalogue (Vienna 1983), No. 12/4.

21   Rotraud Bauer and Herbert Haupt, *Das Kunstkammerinventar Kaiser Rudolfs II, 1607–1611* (= *Jahrbuch der Kunsthistorischen Sammlungen in Wien* 72, NF XXXVI, Vienna 1976).

22   Giovanni Benaglia, *Relazione del viaggio fatto a Costantinopoli e ritorno in Germania dell'illustrissimo sig. Conte A. Caprar*, etc., 3rd ed. (Venice 1685); Hammer-Purgstall, op. cit. (note 5), VI, 381–2.

23   Hammer-Purgstall, ibid., VI, 413–15.

24   *Objects for a 'Wunderkammer'*, exhibition catalogue (Colnaghi, London 1981), No. 123.

5

Kilims

It has sometimes been suggested that the Anatolian 'carpets' (Arabic, bisāṭ/plural busuṭ) mentioned by the historians of Mamlūk Egypt and Syria, particularly those from Aksaray, Konya and Karaman, were in fact not pile carpets but flat-weaves; for, among other reasons, the often modest institutions which are said to have possessed them could scarcely have afforded anything grander. Other attributions, to the Hauran in Syria and to Karak and Shawbak in Palestine,[1] and mentions in inventories of estates of deceased persons in the Bursa and Edirne kadis' archives, suggesting that kilims were also made in Thrace and the Balkans, seem to complicate the picture. But although we now naturally think of Anatolia as the home of the kilim, there are no technical reasons why local demand for these often handsome floor-coverings should not have been locally satisfied. However, the descriptions of them in the sources, mostly giving ground colours ('red', 'white', 'blue'), are, unfortunately, far too schematic to give an idea of local patterns.

The earliest record of kilims grouped by provenance so far published is the Istanbul list of fixed prices and services (narḥ defteri) for 1640,[2] which includes floor kilims, 'mule' kilims and 'camel' kilims from Selendi, Kula in Germiyan, Demirci and Yassıyurd, all but the last, which may be a trade name, well-known centres of pile-carpet production – pale blue (māī), red, red and green or striped (ālāca) – pricing them, evidently by their dimensions: the absence of further descriptions is an indication that patterns of local types were already standardized (cf. p. 37). The kilims listed are relatively expensive, particularly compared with felts and even compared with the kilims noted in the contemporary registers of estates from the kadi's court in Edirne.[3] Although these latter contain not a single mention of a kilim by provenance and only rarely even indicate their ground colour, the valuations recorded are fairly standard, at little more than 100 akçe each. Some of the 'camel' kilims in the Istanbul price list are so large and so expensive (a pale-blue kilim measuring more than 7 dhirāʿ [ells] by 6 is priced at 1,030 akçe) would have been

far too large for a camel and the description may therefore be a trade term, having nothing to do with the animal. Alternatively, they and the 'mule' kilims could have been for making up into saddle bags. If it seems significant that the price list confines itself to kilims of Anatolian provenance, it should be remembered that in quite a few respects it is not a complete survey of what was on the Istanbul market in 1640, so that it cannot be taken as evidence that Thracian, Balkan or even Persian kilims could not also be found there.

The general silence of the sources is, however, some indication that in the seventeenth century kilims were still, as it were, in the underworld of textiles, like the cicims and other embroidered wall-hangings or floor-coverings which would inevitably have been a standard item of furnishing for houses in the Ottoman provinces, but which are either ignored entirely or are impenetrably disguised under misleading trade names. This unsatisfactory situation is not confined to Anatolia, for we know even less of the history of the kilim in Iran, and the temptation to assume that the oldest identifiable kilims, which are probably no earlier than the eighteenth century, continue local styles and patterns that had become standardized centuries before, is one that should be resisted. In fact, the Anatolian Yürüks and Türkmen were, as Halil Inalcık has shown,[4] the object of continual interference from the Ottoman central authorities. Even if it makes much sense, therefore, to speak of discrete tribes and tribal groups of kilims in Anatolia, their appearance could have changed considerably and radically before the eighteenth century; the weavers could easily have reacted to patterns brought in from outside; and they could easily have assimilated entirely the traditional patterns of another tribal group. This was all the more the case with urban centres like Konya or Kayseri, where kilims were manufactured to order as a cottage industry in response to market demand, producing goods for merchants to export elsewhere and changing patterns accordingly. This situation is, of course, now distorted by the growth of mass production of kilims for export to foreign markets which order them by type of pattern. The practice has led recently to an artificial stantardization of types, each of which may be given a trade name or toponym by which to identify it; historically, however, such a method can only be misleading.

The situation changes when we come to consider the impact of kilims on the luxury market, less the brilliant tapestry-woven productions with silk and with metal thread made for the Safavid Court, associated with Kashan in the late-sixteenth and early-seventeenth centuries,[5] than a series of Anatolian kilims of the same period which have recently come to notice and which have been classified, without exaggeration, as 'Palace' kilims. They mostly seem to have been large and, to judge from a fragment datable *c*.1600 from the Eşrefoğlu mosque in Beyşehir (now in the Mevlânâ Museum in Konya), were, unlike pile carpets, indebted to a considerable extent to textile designs. The fragment has an ogival pattern with medallion filling and a double hastate border.[6] Of even greater interest are recently published kilim fragments from the Great Mosque at Divriği in Central Anatolia.[7] Their fragmentary state long precluded analysis of the patterns, but they have now been restored and are a principal feature of the Vakıflar Carpet Museum in the basement of the Sultan's apartments in the mosque of Sultan Ahmed in Istanbul. Their edgings are similar to those of the Beyşehir kilim, with a hastate counterchange, but with a principal border of cartouches and rosettes and a field of dense lotus-rosettes and spiralling tulip-scrolls on a dark ground. Others have designs of curling feathery (*ṣāz*) leaves and hastate or joggled borders very reminiscent of Egyptian Mamlūk architectural decoration of the late fifteenth century.

Far better preserved is a large kilim in the Bayerisches Armeemuseum in Ingolstadt,[8] evidently booty from one of the series of defeats sustained by the Ottoman armies following the Relief of Vienna in 1683 and shown now with the tent of the Grand Vizier Süleymān Paşa which was captured at Mohács in 1687. This example has floral borders and a field with densely repeating floral sprigs. The Vienna campaign of 1683 was, as noted above (cf. p. 144), almost certainly a conscious replay of Süleymān the Magnificent's siege of Vienna in 1529, and the kilim may even have been chosen as an antique 'stage prop' with associations of Süleymān the Magnificent, to lend realism (if that is the word) to Ḳara Muṣṭafā Paşa's advance on Vienna.

As for the dating of the other kilims of this type, it is certainly significant that the Great Mosque at Divriği bears a restoration inscription of Süleymān the Magnificent, dated 93– AH (the last digit is illegible), i.e. some time during the period 1523–33.[9] At Beyşehir, in and

adjacent to the Eşrefoğlu mosque, there were also building works in the same century, including a restoration inscription dated 982/1574–5 in the name of Muṣṭafā Beg, son of a vizier (*vazīr-i Sulṭānī*), as well as a mausoleum dated 969/1561–2.[10] A further kilim similar in technique and design has also come to light in the Yörgüç Paşa mosque at Gümüş, near Gümüshacıköy in the vilayet of Amasya, which was restored by the vizier Rüstem Paşa in 968/1560–1.[11] This strongly suggests, without, however, being conclusive proof, that the 'Court' kilims were an innovation of the later sixteenth century.

Belkis Balpınar[12] has identified a further fragment of a large kilim, now in the Vakıflar Carpet Museum in Istanbul, with overall sprigged decoration somewhat similar to that of the Ingolstadt example, but on a red ground. This, and a few other kilims of different types, like one with bands of fan-like carnations from the Hisar Bey mosque at Kütahya,[13] may well date from the early-seventeenth century. Other recent discoveries include a prayer kilim with side columns, branched carnations in the spandrels, a hanging flask in the niche and an inscription panel of Persian blessings above.[14] Possibly the most important, however, for the purposes of establishing provenance, is a kilim in the Kestner Museum, Hamburg (NO.5424),[15] made up of fragments of another large kilim sewn together. The central medallion has a cherry-red ground and a rich filling of florists' flowers, characteristic of carpets of Cairene manufacture of the later sixteenth and the seventeenth centuries. This has suggested that the kilims too were woven in Cairo and, among other technical peculiarities which distinguish them from many Anatolian groups, they tend to show the use of S-spun wool, which is infrequent outside Egypt. That said, the designs of these 'Court' kilims are for the most part closer to textiles or to the medallions and crenellations of appliqué tent-work. This is, in a way, not surprising since, as the Ingolstadt kilim demonstrates, such kilims were particularly associated with Ottoman campaign tents.

Further research and field work will probably bring more of these grand kilims to light and show how and when they came to be manufactured. It is, however, rather extraordinary that such an obvious achievement in design should have had so little apparent effect on the less pretentious kilims of Anatolia. The prayer kilim, for example, in the Topkapı Saray collections (*No. 41* in the present volume) is, in contrast, much closer in appearance to pile prayer rugs from South-West Anatolia or the Uşak area.

The other Anatolian kilims illustrated (*Nos. 42–45*) are of nineteenth-century date and come from the Misbah Muhayyeş collection. They are representative

147

of local nomad types, woven on easily transportable looms, that are made as narrow strips which are then sewn together. Most of them are from the Afshar nomad confederation of Eastern Anatolia, using the wool from their own flocks, and made for daily use, with dyes prepared according to traditional recipes, and having designs with stylized motifs which may originally have had symbolic significance.

NOTES TO CHAPTER 5

1 Donald P. Little, 'Data from the Haram documents on rugs in late 14th century Jerusalem' in Robert Pinner and Walter B. Denny (eds.), *Carpets of the Mediterranean countries 1400–1600* (London 1986), 83–93.

2 M. S. Kütükoğlu, *Osmanlılarda narh müessesesi ve 1640 narh defteri* (Istanbul 1983), 178–85.

3 Ö. L. Barkan, 'Edirne askerî kassam'ına ait tereke defterleri (1545–1659)', *Belgeler* III (Ankara 1966), 1–479.

4 Halil Inalcık, 'The Yürüks: Their origins, expansion and economic role' in *Carpets of the Mediterranean countries*, op. cit., 39–65.

5 Cf. F. Spuhler, 'Der figurale Kaschen-Wirkteppich aus den Sammlungen der regierenden Fürsten von Liechtenstein', *Kunst des Orients* V/1 (1968), 55–61.

6 Şerare Yetkin, 'Türk kilim sanatında yeni bir gurup, Saray kilimleri', *Belleten* XXXV/138 (Ankara 1971), 217–27.

7 Belkis Acar (Balpınar), 'Divriği Ulu Camii'ndeki halı ve kilimler' in *Divriği Ulu Camii ve Darüşşifası* (Ankara 1978), 159–228; cf.

Charles Grant Ellis, 'The rugs from the Great Mosque of Divriği', *Halı* LI/3 (1978), 269–74

8 *Osmanisch-Türkisches Handwerk aus süddeutschen Sammlungen*, exhibition catalogue (Munich 1979), No. 1 (Ingolstadt, Bayerisches Armeemuseum, A.1855, 580 × 480 cm); Şerare Yetkin, 'Osmanlı Saray sanatı üslubundaki kilimlerden yeni iki örnek', *Vakıflar Dergisi* XIII (1981), 375–86.

9 M. van Berchem, *Corpus Inscriptionum Arabicarum: 3, Asie Mineure* (Cairo 1910), 83–5.

10 Şerare Yetkin, art. cit. (note 8).

11 Ibid.

12 Belkis Balpınar, 'Klassische Kelims', *Halı* VI/1 (1983), 13–20; ead., with Udo Hirsch, *Flatweaves of the Vakıflar Museum, Istanbul* (Wesel 1979).

13 Şerare Yetkin, art. cit. (note 6).

14 Y. Petsopoulos, *Kilims. The art of tapestry weaving in Anatolia, the Caucasus and Persia* (London and New York 1979), Fig. 61.

15 Ibid., Fig. 60; Belkis Balpınar, art. cit. (note 12).

Illustrations 46–98:
PERSIAN, CAUCASIAN AND CENTRAL ASIAN CARPETS

CAPTIONS AND NOTES TO ILLUSTRATIONS
46–98

46   Floral rug (detail), one of a pair, warps blue cotton, wefts ivory-coloured cotton, Persian knot, 48 knots per square cm, pile wool, Iran, nineteenth century (Isfahan); 13/2226 (A.11667). Dimensions 200 × 140 cm overall.
The field is a lattice of floral lozenges, each with a filling of rather naturalistic roses. The border is a chain-scroll of roses and other more or less naturalistic flowers. The guard stripes are undulating floral scrolls.

47   Rug (detail), warps and wefts if ivory-coloured cotton, Turkish knot, 16 knots per square cm, pile wool, Iran, nineteenth century (Isfahan); 13/2260 (A.11701). Dimensions 257 × 111 cm overall.
The field has an 8-lobed medallion with composite stylized lotus buds, the lobed corner-pieces being treated as quarter-medallions. The ground is a spiralling scroll with running or leaping animals – rabbits, hounds, deer and foxes – and the heads of dragons and other monsters, a reminiscence of the classical Islamic animal *wāqwāq* scroll. The lotus-buds in the corner-pieces contain small birds. The borders and guard stripes are of angular undulating floral scrollwork.

48   Prayer rug (detail), one of a pair, warps blue wool, wefts ivory-coloured cotton, Persian knot, 36 knots per square cm, pile wool, Iran, nineteenth century (Isfahan); 13/2007 (A,11648). Dimensions 228 × 140 cm overall.
The field is a mihrab niche with lobed arch, decorative capitals and black side columns, filled with an enormous decorated vase containing a large bouquet and with flowering branches, some of them with birds (pheasant, doves, jays, etc.) characteristic of sixteenth-century Safavid ornament. The spandrels have a palmette filling with further flowering sprays on a contrasting ground. The border is of birds and animals couchant, some confronted some addorsed, among flowering plants. The guard stripes are running scrolls, a sort of double meander.

49   Medallion rug (detail), warps pink or occasionally undyed fawn wool, wefts undyed fawn wool, Persian knot, 16 knots per square cm, pile wool, Caucasus, nineteenth century (Shirvan, or some Iranian centre after a Shirvan prototype); 13/2206 (A.11647). Dimensions 265 × 143 cm overall.
The field has three lozenge medallions with hooked outlines, each having a cruciform filling of smaller composite medallions, buds, hooks and florets. The ground is filled with hooked lozenges, rosettes, stylized birds and animals, hooks and comb-like motifs. The corner-pieces have cross-shaped medallions and lozenge filling. The border is a series of hooked lozenges with bars between, a sort of laxer version of the Caucasian 'crab' motif. The guard stripes are chains of tiny lozenges.

50   Medallion rug (detail), warps and wefts of ivory-coloured cotton, Turkish knot, 16 knots per square cm, pile wool, Iran, nineteenth century (Gorovan type, woven in the villages round about Herez in Persian Azerbaijan); 13/2237 (A.11678). Dimensions 210 × 123 cm overall.
The field has a central 8-petalled medallion with an irregular 8-pointed star at the centre and floral filling; above and below are bold finials. The ground is of branched stems with serrated 'oak-leaves' and small blossoms. The border is a chain of fringed kite-like palmettes with lax floral stems between them. The guard stripes are of undulating floral scroll.

51   Medallion rug, warps and wefts ivory-coloured cotton, Turkish knot, 16 knots per square cm, pile wool, Iran, nineteenth century; 13/2256 (A.11697). Dimensions 195 × 131 cm.
The field has a central lozenge medallion, cropped at the sides, with deeply serrated contours, filled with vertical chains of 8-petalled rosettes. The similarly serrated corner-pieces also have rosette filling, though the chains are not so obvious. The ground of the medallion is decorated with large star-flowers. The border is an angular undulating scroll with feathery leaves and star-flowers. The guard bands are of undulating trefoil scroll.

52   Prayer rug (detail), warps and wefts undyed café-au-lait wool, Turkish knot, 16 knots per square cm, pile wool, probably Caucasian, nineteenth century; 13/2225. Dimensions 221 × 159 cm.
The field is nearly symmetrical with a niche with pointed stepped arches at either end and schematized side columns or consoles between. At the centre is a star-medallion with pendants or finials compartmented to give a stepped rosette at the centre with palmettes and other motifs in the cells around it. The effect is curiously reminiscent of the shrine and ambulatory used to decorate one of the Palace carpets (cf. *No. 29*), and may well be intended to represent one of the great Shīʿī shrines, at Najaf, Kerbela or Meshed. The ground is also compartmented, including rosettes and hands, the *pençe* or so-called 'hand of Fāṭima', in Islam a common sign against the evil eye. The spandrels or corner-pieces are filled with large palmettes. The border is an angular undulating scroll with guard stripes of rosettes or foliate motifs in running scrolls.

53   Medallion rug (detail), warps pale-blue cotton, wefts ivory-coloured cotton, Persian knot, 64 knots per square cm,

pile wool, Iran, nineteenth century (Kashan); 13/2245 (A.11686). Dimensions 202 × 132 cm overall.

The field has a central stepped lozenge medallion with composite palmettes as pendants or finials. At the centre is a composite 8-petalled rosette from which spring stems with polychrome lotuses and naturalistic flowers to fill the remainder of the lozenge. The lobed corner-pieces are treated somewhat similarly to quarter-medallions, but their floral filling, of fan-shaped carnations or Sweet Sultan (*Centaurea*), is more naturalistic. The sides are also lobed and have pairs of bold tulip-like flowers. The border is an undulating scroll with lotus-heads and dense floral stems. The guard stripes are of undulating floral scroll. The field ground is of many-flowered stems springing from the palmette finials.

54 Medallion rug (detail), warps undyed fawn wool or cream and green cotton, wefts cream wool, Turkish knot, 9 knots per square cm, pile wool, Western Iran (possibly Hamadan), nineteenth century; 13/2228 (A.11669). Dimensions 195 × 109 cm overall.

The field has a central medallion with tall finials and at the centre a lozenge with a surround of linked foliate motifs. The angular corner-pieces with similar filling are treated more or less as quarter-medallions. The border is of foliate heads linked by angular stems and vertical pinnate leaves to form a running scroll.

55 Rug, warps blue cotton, wefts white cotton, Persian knot, 56 knots per square cm, pile wool, Iran, nineteenth century (Tabriz); 13/2238 (A.11679). Dimensions 192 × 126 cm.

The field has a central stepped lozenge medallion with a finial at each tip, those on the vertical axis being larger and each enclosing an 8-petalled rosette; the lobed corner-pieces are treated as quarter-lozenges. The ground and the filling of the medallion are of lozenges containing rosettes with chinoiserie lotuses at their tips and with feathery leaves and smaller rosettes between them. The border is of stylized lotus-heads joined by angular stems giving the effect of a jerky double undulating scroll. The guard stripes are of thin undulating floral scrolls.

56 Floral rug (detail), warps blue cotton, wefts ivory-coloured cotton, Persian knot, 24 knots per square cm, pile wool, Iran, nineteenth century; 13/2257 (A.11698). Dimensions 200 × 128 cm overall.

The field has a central cropped lozenge medallion with serrated outline and arrow-shaped finials and a floral filling, with angular corner-pieces similarly filled. The ground is a rectangular lattice of lozenge rosettes linked by stiff leaves and florets. The border is an angular undulating scroll with leafy stems, stylized lotus-heads and other flowers. The guard stripes are of undulating scrolls.

As the result of careless washing, the reds have run.

57 Rug, warps and wefts of undyed cream wool, Persian knot, 16 knots per square cm, pile wool, Iran, nineteenth

century (Feraghan); 13/2211 (A.11652). Dimensions 188 × 121 cm.

The field is of parallel stripes of alternating cloud-bands and clip motifs separated by narrower bands of dotted zigzag. The border is composed of four overrunning angular scrolls punctuated by large foliate heads. The guard stripes are an undulating lotus-scroll.

58 Carpet fragment (detail), warps and wefts yellow wool, Persian knot, 80 knots per square cm, pile wool enhanced with metal thread, North-West Iran, possibly Tabriz, seventeenth century; 13/1890. Dimensions 234 × 160 cm overall.

The field has a central 8-pointed star with lobed contours and an 8-petalled rosette at the centre; the filling of both is bichrome split palmette scrolls in contrasting colours on contrasting grounds. The corner-pieces are quarter-stars, but with more detailed split palmettes on a ground of fine lotus-scroll. The ground of the field is swirling spiral lotus-scrolls with discrete cloud-bands. The border design features alternating oblong cartouches and rosettes, the cartouches bearing *nasta'līq* verses, one line to a cartouche but sequentially arranged in pairs; the verses have been identified as from the *Divan* of Ḥāfiẓ. The fawn ground is decorated overall with fine lotus-scrolls picked out in white with black and crimson accents (compare the spandrel filling of *No. 25*). The guard stripes appear to be a meander.

Some of the motifs and some of the colour-scheme are shared with the large sixteenth-century Uşak carpets made for the Ottoman Court. Most of the motifs and the colour-scheme in general are also shared with the Court carpets illustrated in the present volume (*Nos. 2–35*), which are generally agreed to have been woven in the nineteenth century. It does not, of course, necessarily follow that, despite its convincingly antique appearance, the present piece was also woven in the nineteenth century, for there is a series of properly documented inscription carpets from Tabriz in comparable style and dating from the later sixteenth and the seventeenth centuries. However, it does suggest how craftsmen with little imagination or time to think might have found some of their designs used for the nineteenth-century Palace carpets close at hand.

59 Runner (detail), flat-woven, wool, made as a single piece, Iran, nineteenth century (Shiraz, probably Qashghai nomad work); 13/2045. Dimensions 625 × 161 cm overall.

60 Floral runner, warps and wefts cream-coloured undyed wool, Turkish knot, 36 knots per square cm, pile wool, Caucasus, nineteenth century (Zeyhur/Sejshour–Kuba); 13/2197 (A.11633), Dimensions 297 × 85 cm.

The field is covered with ranks of roses and shows Russian influence. The piece was doubtless woven for the Russian market.

61 Runner (detail), warps white wool, wefts undyed fawn wool, Turkish knot, 24 knots per square cm, pile wool,

Northern Caucasus, nineteenth century (Kuba); 13/2036. Dimensions 244 × 94 cm overall.

The star motifs which fill the field are characteristic of Lezghian design, in which the centres are often barred crosses as seen here. The filling is of rosettes and stylized foliate motifs. The border is a double meander. The guard stripes are of rosettes.

62 Geometric medallion rug (detail), warps and wefts of cream wool, Turkish knot, 16 knots per square cm, pile wool, Caucasus, late eighteenth–nineteenth century (Shirvan); 13/2244 (A.11685). Dimensions 161 × 98 cm overall.

The field consists of a horizontally symmetrical indented panel of three large lozenge medallions filled with hooked crosses, linked by pairs of small lozenges and on a ground of starry blossoms. The ground of the panel and the indentations are filled with comb-like motifs and repeated hooked triangles. The border is a zigzag of angular serrated leaves alternating with motifs resembling tuning forks. The guard stripes are of repeated 8-petalled rosettes.

A Shirvan geometric carpet incorporating many of the same motifs is in the Metropolitan Museum, New York, 22.100.4; cf. M. Dimand and Jean Mailey, *Oriental rugs in the Metropolitan Museum of Art*, op. cit., No. 174.

63 Medallion rug, warps and wefts of ivory-coloured cotton, Turkish knot, 16 knots per square cm, pile wool, Iran, nineteenth century, Senneh (Sanandaj); 13/2258 (A.11699). Dimensions 182 × 133 cm overall.

The field is a central stepped lozenge medallion with bold barred lozenges at top and bottom in a deeply indented surround. The central lozenge and the surround have a dense rectangular grid of foliate stems and interlacing floral motifs, very characteristic of the Senneh group. The upper and lower lozenges have transverse zigzag bands. The border is of toothed leaves alternating with star-medallions and stylized animals(?), giving an undulating movement. The guard stripes are of tiny rosettes.

64 Geometric rug (detail), warps ivory-coloured cotton, wefts undyed fawn wool, Turkish knot, 24 knots per square cm, pile wool, Caucasus, nineteenth century (Shirvan): 13/2223 (A.11664). Dimensions 246 × 146 cm. overall.

The field contains three large lozenge medallions, arranged vertically, and there is a large lotus or palmette at each end; each lozenge has within it a smaller lozenge in contrasting colours. The blue ground is filled with a variety of small rosettes, lozenges, stars and small geometrically stylized animals. The border is a scroll of alternating S- and Z-motifs connected by angular leaves attached to forked stems. The guard stripes are of wavy scroll.

65 Rug (one of a pair), warps and wefts of ivory-coloured cotton, Persian knot, 24 knots per square cm, pile wool, Caucasus, nineteenth century (Shirvan); 13/2220 (A.11661) Dimensions 165 × 112 cm.

The field design is of staggered rows of angular *boteh* motifs in contrasting colours on a star-studded dark-blue ground, with tassel-like motifs at each side.

The border consists of rectangular compartments filled with stepped triangles, possibly stylized minbars and hanging lamps. The guard stripes are of small repeated 8-petalled rosettes.

Similar *boteh* motifs occur on a prayer rug in the Metropolitan Museum, New York (22.100.3), dated 1223/1808–9; cf. M. Dimand and Jean Mailey, *Oriental rugs in the Metropolitan Museum of Art*, op. cit., No. 171.

66 Rug, warps and wefts of ivory-coloured cotton, Persian knot, 24 knots per square cm, pile wool, Caucasus, nineteenth century (Shirvan); 13/2232 (A.11673). Dimensions 166 × 111 cm.

The field design, which is very similar to that of *No. 65*, is of staggered transverse rows of *boteh* motifs, those with white centres giving a marked diagonal movement. Gaps at the sides, and sometimes between the rows, are filled with assorted motifs, including what appear to be lozenges and stylized letters. The border design consists of stylized pseudo-Kufic, with guard bands of undulating trefoil scrolls.

67 Arabesque rug, warps and wefts of cream wool, Turkish knot, 36 knots per square cm, pile wool, Caucasus, nineteenth century (Shirvan); 13/2212 (A.11653). Dimensions 157 × 133 cm.

The field is an all-over design of transverse bands of broken medallions and stylized floral motifs, including serrated leaves and star flowers, with an edging of crenellations or hastate motifs. The border is of stylized pseudo-Kufic with alternating medallions and interlaces. The guard stripes are of overlapping lozenge chains.

This piece comes from the Misbah Muhayyeş collection; a similar rug is in the collections of the Topkapı Saray proper.

68 Small-pattern floral rug (detail), warps and wefts ivory-coloured cotton, Turkish knot, 24 knots per square cm, pile wool, Caucasus, nineteenth century (Shirvan); 13/2221 (A.11662). Dimensions 159 × 126 cm overall.

The field is a lozenge lattice with large rosettes at the intersections and a filling of stylized chinoiserie lotuses and other smaller flowers. Midway in the overall design, a break in the pattern emphasises the horizontal symmetry. The narrow border is an angular undulating floral scroll.

continued on page 242

48

50

52

54

58

60

61

64

65

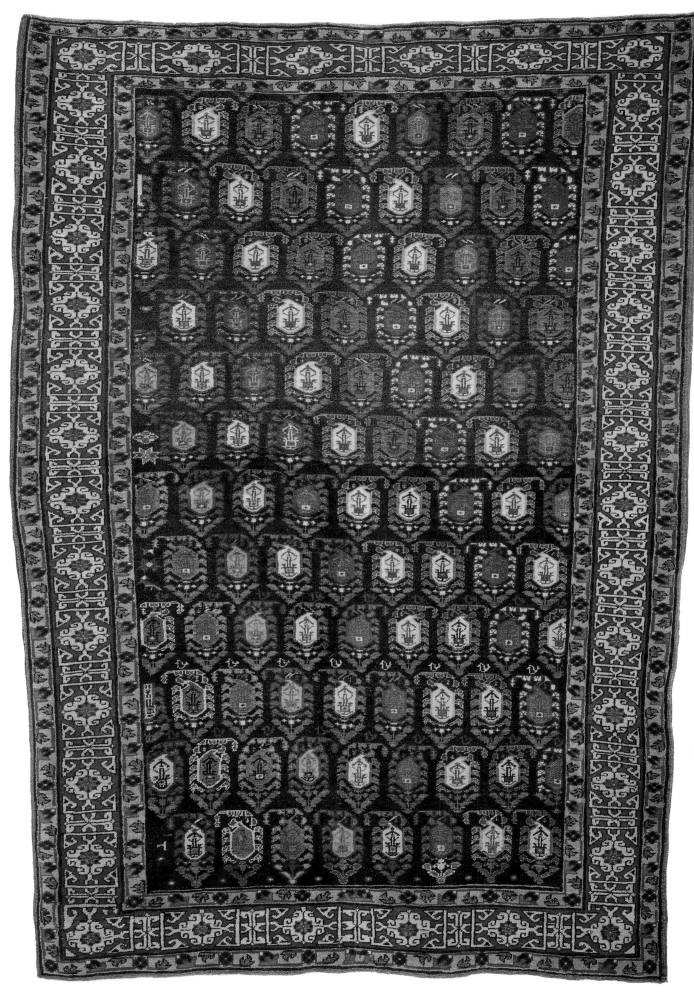

66

69

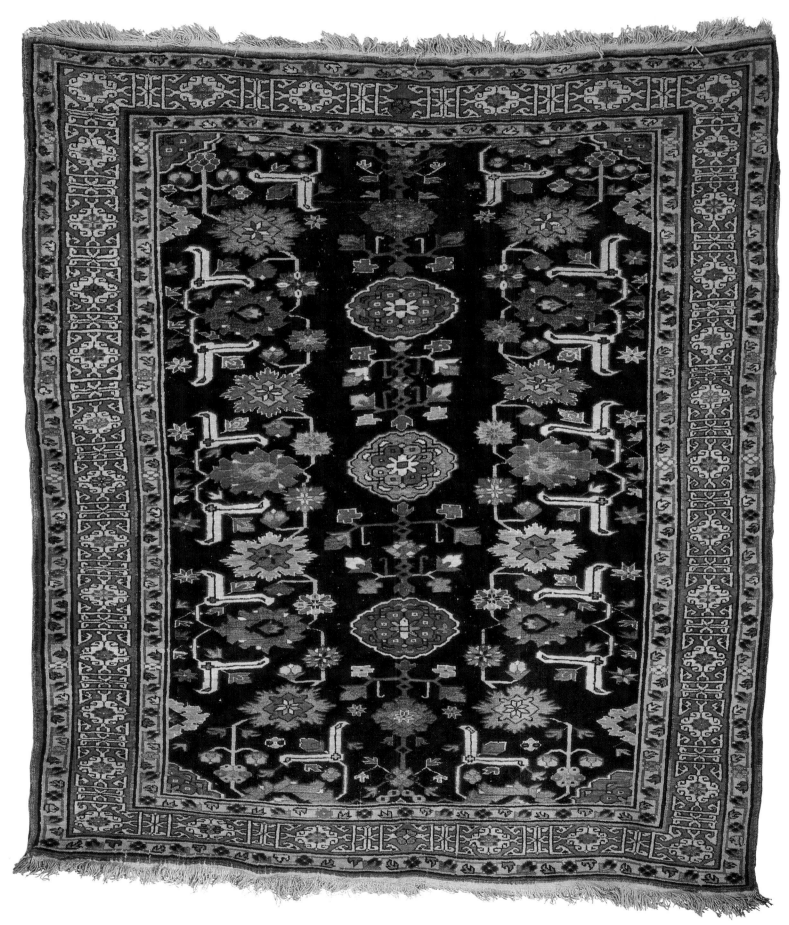

71

73

76

82

84

87

88

90

94

69 Geometric rug, warps and wefts white wool, Turkish knot, 24 knots per square cm, pile wool, Caucasus, nineteenth century (Shirvan); 13/2208 (A.11649). Dimensions 158 × 133 cm.
The field has three large rectangles each containing a hooked lozenge medallion with a central 8-pointed star and stylized birds surrounding each lozenge. On either side of the rectangles and between them are stylized double palmettes on a dark-blue ground studded with lozenges, rosettes, star-like blossoms, and comb motifs. The border is of cropped lozenges with guard stripes of alternating lozenges and bars.

70 Geometric rug, warps and wefts white wool, Turkish knot, 24 knots per square cm, pile wool, Caucasus, nineteenth century (Shirvan); 13/2203 (A.11644). Dimensions 156 × 108 cm.
The field is designed as pairs of panels, the larger rectangles filled with hooked motifs; a row of five stylized crowned insect-like forms fills the space at either end. The ground is scattered with rosettes, lozenges and small quadrupeds. The border is of contrasting paired hooked rosettes, flanked by guard bands of continuous stylized florets.

71 Carpet (one of a pair), warps white cotton, wefts cream-coloured wool, Turkish knot, 24 knots per square cm, pile wool, Shirvan, nineteenth century; 13/2216 (A.11657). Dimensions 154 × 137 cm.
The field has a central strip of rosettes alternating with knotted floral sprays, with on either side strips of stylized lotuses, feathery petalled rosettes and smaller starry floral motifs bracketed by pairs of split palmettes. At each corner there is a small quarter-medallion. The stylized pseudo-Kufic border, a frequently occurring feature of Shirvan rugs, is evidently of Anatolian derivation, as may well be some of the floral motifs in the present example. The guard stripes are an angular double undulating scroll.

72 Geometric rug (detail), warps pink wool, wefts white wool, Turkish knot, 16 knots per square cm, pile wool, Caucasus, nineteenth century (Kuba or Shirvan); 13/2016. Dimensions 203 × 132 cm overall.
The field has a staggered design of angular palmettes, each on a single stem flanked by pairs of angular palmettes and hook-shaped leaves. The filling is of addorsed stylized quadrupeds.

73 Rug, warps and wefts undyed fawn wool, Turkish knot, 9 knots per square cm, pile wool, Central Asia, nineteenth

century (Beshir–Ersari); 13/2247 (A.11688). Dimensions 173 × 115 cm.
The entire field is divided into bold lozenges separated by lozenge bands; each principal lozenge is filled with a cruciform motif having a quadruple lozenge at the centre and serrated rectangular arms, the whole suggesting a floral motif. The border is of chains of lozenges in groups, alternately larger and smaller. The guard bands are of continuous small hastate motifs.

74 Kilim (detail), wool, made in two narrow strips which have then been sewn together, the flat-woven field embroidered with repeating motifs, Caucasus, nineteenth century; 13/2262 (A.11703). Dimensions 232 × 184 cm overall.

75 Runner (one of a pair), warps and wefts white cotton, Turkish knot, 16 knots per square cm, pile wool, Iran, early nineteenth century (Hamadan); 13/2196 (A.11632). Dimensions 505 × 100 cm.

76 Runner (one of a pair), warps and wefts cream-coloured undyed wool, Turkish knot, 12 knots per square cm, pile wool, Iran, nineteenth century (Hamadan); 13/2198 (A.11635). Dimensions 390 × 95 cm.
The field contains cropped lozenges with serrated borders; alternate lozenges are filled with rosettes and with hachuring similar to that of the ground. Separately woven strips have been added at each end.

77 Narrow rug (detail), warps and wefts ivory-coloured cotton, Turkish knot, 12 knots per square cm pile wool, Iran, early nineteenth century (Hamadan- 'Mosul' type); 13/2259 (A.11700). Dimensions 184 × 88 cm overall.
The field is occupied by transverse rows of floral motifs, including *botehs* on short stems, on a plain red ground. The border is a series of 6-petalled rosettes on an ivory-white ground. The guard bands are of smaller rosettes on a brown ground.

78 Garden rug (detail), warps and wefts ivory-coloured cotton, Turkish knot, 16 knots per square cm, pile wool, Iran, nineteenth century (Hamadan); 13/2213 (A.11654). Dimensions 199 × 144 cm.
The field has staggered rows of cypresses standing in schematic medallions and on inverted cloud-bands, alternating with highly stylized trees of life flanked by confronted birds. Between the rows of cypresses are staggered rows of blossoming trees on a ground of scattered flowers and stylized insects. The border is a stiff scroll of alternating lozenges and rosettes. The guard stripes are of undulating trefoil scroll.
The most famous examples of carpets of this pattern are a series made for the tomb of Shah 'Abbās at Qum, one of which is signed by the craftsman Ni'matallāh and is dated 1082/1671–2. His *nisba* is Jawshaqānī, from Jawshaqan in the Isfahan oasis, where carpets were evidently already being woven at this time. It was a carpet-weaving centre from the

eighteenth to the present century, though in the trade the name is often given to any rugs exhibiting particular designs, but not necessarily from Jawshaqan itself.

79 Floral carpet (detail), warps beige cotton, wefts ivory-coloured cotton, Turkish knot, 16 knots per square cm, pile wool, Iran, nineteenth century; 13/2046. Dimensions 310 × 270 cm overall.

The field is decorated with schematized lotus-heads, trefoils and feathery leaves radiating outwards from a central 8-petalled rosette. The border is a double undulating foliate scroll with large rosettes and lotuses. The guard stripes are triple bands of beading, meander and 4-part lozenges alternating with St Andrew's crosses.

80 Medallion rug (detail), warps and wefts ivory-coloured cotton, Turkish knot, 16 knots per square cm, pile wool, Iran, nineteenth century (Hamadan); 13/2253 (A.11694). Dimensions 188 × 143 cm overall.

The field is designed as a niche, almost symmetrically, with identical lobed corner-pieces, but with the medallion placed below centre: it is thus of pointed lobed ovoid shape, with a conspicuous lotus finial at each end. It encloses an 8-petalled rosette with floral filling. The corner-pieces contain quarter-flowers. The ground is of floral stems. The border is an angular undulating scroll with stylized floral heads, and the guard bands consist of undulating scrolls.

81 Rug (detail), warps blue cotton, wefts ivory-coloured cotton, Turkish knot, 16 knots per square cm, pile wool, Iran, nineteenth century (Hamadan); 13/2229 (A.11670). Dimensions 203 × 107 cm.

The field is treated as a stepped niche, almost symmetrical above and below, with indentations in the sides. The central medallion is also almost symmetrical on both axes and is filled with stylized lotus-stems, with 8-petalled rosettes and feathery leaves. Above and below the medallion there is a finial or pendant: these divide the ground vertically, the space around them being filled with flowering stems and heavy serrated leaves. The whole niche is then set in a rectangular frame with a ground of floral trails. The angular undulating scroll border is of stylized chinoiserie lotus-heads. The guard stripes consist of thin hachuring.

82 Rug (detail), warps and wefts ivory-coloured cotton, Turkish knot, 16 knots per square cm, pile wool, Iran, nineteenth century (Hamadan); 13/2243 (A.11675). Dimensions 200 × 130 cm overall.

The field is horizontally symmetrical, with an angular pointed arch at each end; the central lozenge medallion has, above and below it, a vertical chain of smaller lozenge medallions which recur as half-lozenges down each side of the field. All these motifs have spikes or arrow-shaped projections. The filling is of angular foliate motifs and stylized birds, the corner-pieces being treated as quarter-medallions. The border is made up of repeated stylized foliate motifs, while the guard stripes are of repeated stylized florets.

83 Medallion rug (detail), warps and wefts ivory-coloured cotton, Turkish knot, 16 knots per square cm, pile wool, Iran, nineteenth century (Hamadan, under Caucasian influence); 13/2219 (A.11660). Dimensions 192 × 132 cm overall.

In the centre of the field there is a medallion with leafy projections, hook-like tentacles and an elaborate finial or pendant above and below; the similarly decorated corner-pieces are in the form of quarter-medallions. At the centre of the medallion there is an 8-petalled rosette. The border is of foliate or floral heads joined by thin stems to form a double undulating scroll. The guard stripes are of hooked *boteh* motifs forming a chain.

84 Medallion rug (detail), warps and wefts ivory-coloured cotton, Turkish knot, 15 knots per square cm; pile wool, Iran, nineteenth century (Hamadan, under Caucasian influence); 13/2233 (A.11674). Dimensions 200 × 127 cm overall.

The composition is very similar to that of *No. 83*, the central medallion having bold finials and hooked appendages enclosing an 8-petalled rosette with floral filling. The corner-pieces are treated as quarters of the medallion together with the finial, thus giving the sides a jagged outline. The border is of lotus- or palmette-medallions linked by angular stems with dense florets – in effect a jerky multiple undulating scroll.

85 Medallion rug (detail), warps and wefts ivory-coloured cotton, Turkish knot, 24 knots per square cm, pile wool, Iran, nineteenth century (Hamadan); 13/2222 (A.11663). Dimensions 202 × 138 cm overall.

The field has a large lobed medallion with beaded border, conspicuous finials and floral filling around a central 8-petalled rosette. The corner-pieces have lobed outlines and are filled with floral stems springing from the corners. The ground is of dense stems with small flowers. The border is an undulating scroll made up of long palmettes with elaborate tendril tips.

86 Medallion rug (detail), warps and wefts cream-coloured cotton, Turkish knot, 16 knots per square cm, pile wool, Iran, nineteenth century (probably Hamadan); 13/2210 (A.11651). Dimensions 195 × 120 cm overall.

The field has a central lobed medallion with a finial or pendant above and below; the lobed corner-pieces are in the form of quarter-medallions. These elements are all bordered by feathery leaves or swags: internally they are compartmented and filled with stylized chinoiserie lotuses, roses and other flowers. The ground is densely worked with floral scrollwork set with larger lozenge-shaped rosettes. The border is an angular undulating scroll with *boteh* motifs. The guard stripes are of narrower undulating scroll with similar but smaller *botehs*.

The pile, particularly at the centre, shows heavy wear.

87 Rug, warps and wefts ivory-coloured cotton, Turkish knot, 16 knots per square cm, pile wool, Iran, nineteenth

century (Hamadan); 13/2243 (A.11684). Dimensions
170 × 95 cm.
The field is a dense rectangular lattice of lozenges and floral motifs; these are drawn in black, and in many places the fibres have rotted. The angular corner-pieces continue the design, but use a contrasting ground colour.

88   Runner (detail), warps and wefts undyed fawn wool, Turkish knot, 12 knots per square cm, pile wool, Iran, nineteenth century (Hamadan–'Mosul' type); 13/2239 (A.11680). Dimensions 340 × 152 cm overall.

89   Runner (detail), warps pink wool, wefts undyed fawn wool, Turkish knot, 12 knots per square cm, pile wool, Iran, nineteenth century (Hamadan–'Mosul' type); 13/2255 (A.11696). Dimensions 327 × 139 cm overall.
The field is of branched cruciform motifs separated by groups of stylized leaves in pairs. The border is an angular undulating scroll with hooked leaves. The guard stripes are a running floral scroll.

90   Floral rug (detail), warps blue cotton, wefts ivory-coloured cotton, Persian knot, 42 knots per square cm, pile wool, Iran, nineteenth century (Sarouk); 13/2235 (A.11676). Dimensions 200 × 121 cm overall.
The field is an all-over lozenge grid filled with transverse rows or chains of lotus-rosettes and other flowers. The border design consists of a stiffly undulating scroll featuring pinnate leaves and small flowers. The guard stripes are undulating scrolls.

91   Medallion rug (detail), warps and wefts of ivory-coloured cotton, Persian knot, 36 knots per square cm, pile wool, Iran, nineteenth century (Sarouk); 13/2242 (A.11683). Dimensions 204 × 120 cm overall.
The field has a central star-medallion with serrated contours and floral filling; it encloses a pointed lobed medallion with a central 8-petalled rosette. The ground is of vertical branched stems with lotus-heads with trailing stems of other florets. The corner-pieces are small, each having a lotus-head pointing into the corner. At the base of the field there is a row of candle-like flowers. The border is a chain of medallions and 4-petalled rosettes on a dense floral ground. The guard stripes are of undulating floral scroll.

92   Medallion rug (detail), warps pale-blue cotton, wefts white cotton, Persian knot, 64 knots per square cm, pile wool, Iran, nineteenth century (Sarouk); 13/2218 (A.11659). Dimensions 203 × 126 cm overall.
The field has a central 8-pointed star-medallion with long finials above and below; a large rosette at the centre has cruciform floral filling and the space surrounding it is filled with dense flowering stems and lotus-heads. Each of the small, lobed corner-pieces is broken by a decorated vase from which issue the floral stems that make up the ground decoration. At the sides there are further half-vases from which other stems issue. The border is of alternating

medallions and 4-petalled rosettes. The guard stripes are thin bands of lozenges.

93   Medallion rug (detail), warps blue cotton, wefts ivory-coloured cotton, Persian knot, 36 knots per square cm, pile wool, Iran, nineteenth century (Hamadan–Sarouk); 13/2250 (A.11691). Dimensions 200 × 142 cm overall.
The field has a central lobed lozenge medallion, within which are concentric lozenges and a central 8-petalled rosette; the filling consists of floral stems and serrated leaves. The lobed corner-pieces have irregular palmette-heads and straight flowering stems. The ground is of laxer flowering stems with large feathery or serrated leaves, singly or in pairs. The border is an undulating scroll with feathery leaves and alternating lozenges and foliate heads. The guard band is a double-stemmed undulating scroll.

94   Medallion rug (detail), warps blue cotton, wefts white cotton, Turkish knot, 36 knots per square cm, pile wool, Iran, nineteenth century (Hamadan–Sarouk); 13/2266 (A.11707). Dimensions 202 × 124 cm overall.
The field has a large medallion with palmette finials; it has a serrated lobed outline and at the centre a many-petalled rosette surrounded by quadripartite floral filling. The lobed corner-pieces have somewhat similar floral filling. The ground is of four stems, two issuing from each end of the field, with dense pairs of serrated leaves and stylized flowers. The border is an angular undulating scroll with shaggy lotus-heads. The guard stripe is of alternating triangles and crosses.

95   Medallion rug (detail), warps blue cotton, wefts ivory-coloured cotton, Turkish knot, 24 knots per square cm, Iran, nineteenth century (Hamadan–Sarouk); 13/2217 (A.11658). Dimensions 203 × 138 cm overall.
The field has a central lozenge medallion with conspicuous finials and, at the centre, an 8-petalled rosette with floral motifs springing from the tip of each petal. The corner-pieces, though more deeply lobed, are effectively treated as quarter-lozenges. The ground is filled with four stems of paired 'oak leaves' and flowers. The border is an undulating scroll with alternating rosettes and large stylized lotus-heads. The guard stripes are stylized bead-and-reel, the beads being *botehs*.

96   Medallion rug (detail), warps blue cotton, wefts ivory-coloured cotton, Turkish knot, 36 knots per square cm, pile wool, Iran, nineteenth century (Sarouk); 13/2254 (A.11695). Dimensions 207 × 130 cm overall.
The field has a large central medallion with stepped outline and buds at each point, and with lobed double finials. This encloses a stepped lozenge filled with an 8-petalled star-rosette. The filling of the medallion like that of the lobed corner-pieces, is a dense network of thin flowered stems. The ground consists of equally dense stylized chinoiserie peony- or lotus-sprays, with stylized horses, with or without riders. The border is made up of foliate heads linked by angular stems to form a multiple undulating scroll. The guard stripes are a running scroll with heart-shaped leaves.

It has been observed that the layout of such carpet designs is somewhat indebted to that of the Safavid 'Portuguese' carpets.

97   Medallion rug (detail), warps and wefts cream-coloured cotton, Turkish knot, 24 knots per square cm, pile wool, Iran, nineteenth century (Hamadan–Sarouk); 13/2240 (A.11631). Dimensions 193 × 145 cm overall.
The field has a central stepped medallion with elaborate pendants, and a stepped lozenge within it has a floral filling and surround and, at the centre, a many-petalled rosette. Each of the heavy stepped corner-pieces is filled with a stylized peacock displaying. The ground is of dense floral stems with conspicuous fan-like carnations, somewhat destroying the balance of medallion and ground. The border is a knotted undulating stem with similar floral decoration. The guard stripes are of hastate motifs.

The considerable differences between this rug and *No. 98* can perhaps be attributed to the influence of foreign rug merchants in Iran during the late nineteenth century: for example, in 1883 the firm of Ziegler opened an office at Arak (formerly Sultanabad) for the mass-production of Sarouk rugs to European taste.

98   Floral rug, (detail), warps blue cotton, wefts white cotton, Persian knot, 56 knots per square cm, pile wool, Iran, nineteenth century (Sarouk, fine quality); 13/2205 (A.11646). Dimensions 192 × 126 cm overall.
The field is a symmetrical niche with cropped angular apices; the central stilted hexagonal medallion has angular finials and a cropped lozenge at the centre. The filling of both is floral, with stylized chinoiserie lotuses, feathery leaves and flowering stems arranged symmetrically on both axes. The ground is of serried transverse rows of complex floral motifs which are picked up, in contrasting colours and on a contrasting white ground, on the surround of the niche. The border is of alternating lobed medallions and undulating rosettes. The guard stripes are undulating scrolls.

Concordance of Topkapı Saray Museum inventory numbers and carpets illustrated in this volume

Topkapı reference	Illustration number	Topkapı reference	Illustration number	Topkapı reference	Illustration number
13/1540	41	13/2042	18	13/2228	54
13/1890	58	13/2043	40	13/2229	81
13/2008	35	13/2044	33	13/2232	66
13/2009	9	13/2045	59	13/2233	84
13/2010	26	13/2046	79	13/2234	82
13/2011	34	13/2157	42	13/2235	90
13/2013	16	13/2158	32	13/2236	37
13/2014	31	13/2160	24	13/2237	50
13/2015	28	13/2161	17	13/2238	55
13/2016	72	13/2162	10	13/2239	88
13/2017	20	13/2163	19	13/2240	97
13/2018	11	13/2196	75	13/2242	91
13/2019	14	13/2197	60	13/2243	87
13/2020	6	13/2198	76	13/2244	62
13/2021	12	13/2203	70	13/2245	53
13/2023	2	13/2205	98	13/2247	73
13/2024	29	13/2206	49	13/2249	38
13/2025	22	13/2207	48	13/2250	93
13/2026	30	13/2208	69	13/2253	80
13/2028	23	13/2210	86	13/2254	96
13/2029	5	13/2211	57	13/2255	89
13/2030	7	13/2212	67	13/2256	51
13/2031	15	13/2213	78	13/2257	56
13/2032	3	13/2216	71	13/2258	63
13/2033	21	13/2217	95	13/2259	77
13/2034	36	13/2218	92	13/2260	47
13/2035	13	13/2219	83	13/2261	43
13/2036	61	13/2220	65	13/2262	74
13/2037	1	13/2221	68	13/2263	44
13/2038	4	13/2222	85	13/2264	45
13/2039	25	13/2223	64	13/2265	39
13/2040	8	13/2225	52	13/2266	94
13/2041	27	13/2226	46		

Index